Telling Life's Tales

A Guide to Writing Life Stories for Print and Publication

Telling Life's Tales

A Guide to Writing Life Stories
for Print and Publication

Sarah-Beth Watkins

**COMPASS
BOOKS**

Winchester, UK
Washington, USA

First published by Compass Books, 2012
Compass Books is an imprint of John Hunt Publishing Ltd., Laurel House, Station Approach,
Alresford, Hants, SO24 9JH, UK
office1@jhpbooks.net
www.johnhuntpublishing.com
www.compass-books.net

For distributor details and how to order please visit the 'Ordering' section on our website.

Text copyright: Sarah-Beth Watkins 2012

ISBN: 978 1 78099 617 2

A CIP catalogue record for this book is available from the British Library.

Design: Stuart Davies

Printed in the USA by Edwards Brothers Malloy

We operate a distinctive and ethical publishing philosophy in all
areas of our business, from our global network of authors to
production and worldwide distribution.

CONTENTS

Chapter Six – Key Elements of Writing

Chapter Seven – Checking the Facts

Chapter Eight – Editing and Presentation

Chapter Twelve – Passing on Your Skills

Dedication

To my Nan, Kathleen Watkins, for all her love and support

Chapter One

What are Life Stories?

What is a Life Story?

We all know what a story is. Our culture has reared us on bedtime stories, stories by the fireside, heroic tales and fantastic retellings of past events. Whether we've read them ourselves or had them read to us, stories have always been a part of our lives. Amongst the stories we are reared on are the stories of our ancestors, their foibles and quirks, and tales of memorable events and occasions that make up our family histories.

These are life stories – the stories that tell us what life was like at a certain time in a certain place. Life stories don't have to stretch back into the dark ages. They could even be of something that happened in the past year but they are someone's experiences written down so that others know what life was like for them. They give us a picture of a slice of life and the people that filled a time and a place through the eyes of an individual, family or organization.

Life stories are not works of fiction, they contain fact. Some people refer to them as life histories which may be more accurate but really they are a mixture of both fact and fiction. They are factual because they are based on the historical events of a life but in the re-telling, they turn into stories, the type that are passed on from generation to generation.

Life stories are a way of recording memories and they are a form of preservation. We nearly all have a relation that we would have loved to know more about; someone who fought in a war, worked hard for a living or travelled abroad at a time when it was rare. There many interesting facts we would love to know about our long gone ancestors. But sometimes we have missed the chance to know more about them and the lives they led.

That's why life-story writing is so important. It is vital to preserve personal histories for family and academic use. We can hardly imagine today what life was like during the Second World War yet it wasn't that long ago. The generation that lived, loved and worked during that time period are dying out and along with them, the first-hand accounts of actually being there, experiencing life in a war-torn world.

It's not just the big events, like enlisting in the Forces, fighting battles and celebrating VE Day, but the smaller things that fascinate us. Nobody had satellite TV, laptop computers or the Internet so what did people do with themselves? They attended tea dances, grew their own vegetables, listened to the radio and children played in the streets when the sirens weren't sounding. When we begin to investigate life's tales, we can be surprised at what we find.

Our lives are so different today that it is hard to imagine living in past circumstances. Reading life stories can take us back to those times and help us to understand what life was really like, the good and the bad, the everyday and the bigger picture.

Can you imagine one of your descendants reading your story a hundred years from now? Think of all the things that will have changed. Wouldn't they love to know what transport we used, how we watched television, what computers were used for?

And it's not just about technology and the fads of the day. Your descendants will want to know how you lived your life. Were you rich or poor? Catholic or Hindu? Were you vegetarian or vegan? Did you live in different countries or travel abroad frequently?

What were the beliefs of the times? We laugh when we think people believed in fairies and put milk out on the windowsill to keep them happy but what will others think of our beliefs a hundred, two hundred, five hundred years down the line?

Writing life stories is a way of saying this is how we were, how we felt, what we believed in and what opinions we held. There is no right or wrong to it. A life contains many elements and it will be up to the reader to decide whether they agree with them or not.

Writing your own life-story and those of others is the ultimate way of preserving personal and family history for other people's pleasure and future generations delight. Telling life's tales is a way of inviting people to find out more about you, your family and the lives you have led. Whether you write a short life-story for a magazine or a book based on your exploits, you are recording your life for other people to read. You will want your readers to laugh with you, cry with you, to enjoy your life's journey or to sympathize with it, bringing your world alive to them. But why write your life's tales? Why should your experiences and those of others go down on paper?

Why Write your Life Story?

We've touched on some reasons why life-story writing is important but there are other, perhaps more personal reasons, why you might want to tell life's tales.

For Your Family

You might want to pass on your history to future generations so that your children's children's children know who you were and what you did. It can be a way of setting the record straight or telling people what really happened in past years. You may want to reveal a family secret or excite your family with amazing historical information you have uncovered. Rather than focusing on yourself, you could also write a family history and compile a book of stories from the past.

To remember People and Places

Life writing is about memory, remembering people and places that have been important in your life. You might want to share your experiences of places you have worked or lived in and likewise, the people that colored your days.

To capture a Specific Time, Job, Role

Life stories can be about a certain time in your life. If you served in the Forces, helped build the Channel Tunnel, sold an invention – these are times when a lot happened to you and you could write about them specifically. Life stories about specific jobs have become popular with subjects such as nursing, midwifery and farming being written about and published.

To record the work of a Company or Business

Have you worked for a famous company? Or started your own unusual business? The history of the company and the work it does may be of interest to others. Histories of companies can be interesting reads especially if the company started out as a small venture and ended up as a multi-national company. Readers can learn from this type of life-story and use the information to make their own businesses successful or to just enjoy a good historical read.

To document the history of a Club or Community Organization

Community clubs can have a long history. They often have local celebrities, genuine community characters and generations of families involved in them. Whether it's a women's group, sports club or local community center, it has a history that people in the area might like to read.

Just to Write

You can decide to write your life-story because you just want to write. Maybe you are new to writing and what better way to start than by writing about the subject you know best – you!

Therapy

Some people write for therapy. There are many life stories in bookshops now that portray a traumatic or highly emotional time in someone's life. Writing your life-story can help you to examine the highs and lows of your years. They can be a way to express emotions that you have never shared with anyone. This can be very therapeutic for the writer but also challenging and emotional. If you are considering this type of writing, be aware that it may affect you and you may need to seek counseling and support.

Types of Life Story

You might have an idea by now of what you would like to write. It could be simply your life from childhood to the present or it could be the history of your local sports team and your involvement in it.

You might have many ideas or few at this stage but let's look now at some different types of life writing to help you along. You will need to decide what type of life-story you want to write before you begin the hard work!

Autobiography

Autobiographies are life histories written by the person who has experienced them.

Biography

Biographies are different in that they are written by someone else. Think of all the celebrity or historical biographies you see in the booksellers – written about a certain character but by a different author.

Joint Ventures

Joint ventures are a bit of both autobiography and biography. They are written by more than one person. For example, they can be a collaboration of two people who have been involved in an organization or club or a husband and wife team writing about their family history.

Memoirs

Memoirs are based more on memory than fact. They are the recollections of the writer. More often, these are written by celebrities about a certain period in their lives.

Diaries

Diaries are dated thoughts and feelings usually written down daily but can be over any given period of time. Usually thought of as more private and revealing than an autobiography.

Collections of Letters

These have seen more popularity in recent years and can give a very real feeling for the times they are written in. They are selected for use in book form from a selection of genuine letters. If you have a hoard of family correspondence buried away, it might be time to dust it off and see what life stories they portray.

Family History

Autobiographies, biographies, memoirs and diaries can all focus on a particular person but they can also portray a family's history. They can focus on a historic connection or years of work in a particular trade.

Fiction and Short Stories

Life writing is factual but you can use elements of it to write fiction. Any writer will bring some of their self to whatever they are writing. For instance, if you were writing a romantic story, you might remember and add in feelings about your first kiss or your last husband! Likewise, a short story written about childhood and growing up in the 1950s might be based on your own upbringing.

Where to find Life Stories

So where do we find life stories and where could you see your story in print? There are five main ways of having your life-story published and read. These are:

- In mainstream book form
- In a magazine
- As a book produced by self-publishing companies
- As a pamphlet or book produced by yourself
- As an e-book

In a Mainstream Book

Life stories are accepted by certain publishers for sale to the mass market. You will need to do some research into the book market to see which publishers are printing autobiographies, biographies and memoirs. Some only publish celebrity works but others will produce life stories if they will appeal to a wide readership. Imagine the sales of *Angela's Ashes by Frank McCourt* or *Suite Française by Irene Nemirovsky.* If you want to see your work in print through a mainstream publisher, you will need to present and market your manuscript. We will give you more help with this later in the book.

In a Magazine

Magazines run life stories every week. Some of them also run monthly life-story specials. Many of the women's magazines actively seek the kind of story which can cover subjects such as relationships, health, children and lifestyles. Other magazines that focus specifically on country life, travel and nostalgia also accept life stories. Have a good look at the magazines on the shelf at your local newsagents and this will point you in the right direction for possible markets. Some of them will expect you to send in a properly presented story, others will ask for your ideas and fill in your story through telephone conversations. Writing for magazines is a good way to start life-story writing and can be very lucrative.

As a book produced by Self-Publishing Companies

Self-publishing companies assist people in seeing their work in print. They will produce your book but at a cost. Some who offer print on demand services can keep the costs down but you must do all your own advertising and promotion. Others will only print x amount of books at y amount of cost.

There are many different companies and it really is a matter of looking around to find the best deal at the fairest price if you choose to take this route. Look in writing magazines such as the *Writing Magazine* and *Writer's Forum* for advertisements for this type of company to see what kind of services they offer.

Doing it Yourself

Today, producing your own book on your own computer has become much easier. You can print off your own copies, design a cover and insert photos or other documents. The costs can be quite high for ink or photocopying but this depends on how many books you want to produce. If you only want to give out copies to your immediate family then this might be the route for you.

For a more professional look, you could take your manuscript to a printers or graphic designer. They can design a cover for you and print out your work on higher-quality paper. Costs again will depend on your budget and the amount printed. However, if you are printing your own work, you must be aware of any legal implications and you will not be able to sell copies without an ISBN number.

As an e-book

It has become much easier today for writers to publish their own work as an e-book. Digital readers are becoming more popular and the reading public can easily download something new to read at the touch of one or two buttons. To produce your own e-book, you will need to be comfortable with using a computer, word-processing, formatting and design. However, if you go through the correct process, you will be able to see your work for sale on websites such as Amazon.

These are just some ways to get your life-story published but there could be other avenues like having a story printed in your local Parish journal, writing a column for a newspaper or sending your story into a publisher to be included in an anthology. We will look more closely at getting published in chapter nine.

Reading Other People's Life Stories

Look at the autobiographies being sold in the shops and browse the appropriate section in your local library. Read a selection of them to get an idea of how other people have written about themselves and what events they have shared.

Some books to include in your reading are:

A Long walk to Freedom: The Autobiography of Nelson Mandela
Call the Midwife by Jennifer Worth
Angela's Ashes by Frank McCourt
Don't Tell Mummy: A True Story of the Ultimate Betrayal by Toni Maguire
Look Back in Hunger by Jo Brand

Dead Woman Pickney: A Memoir of Childhood in Jamaica by
Yvonne Shorter Brown

You will find many others covering different times in history and focusing on people's specific experiences. There are always a lot of celebrity autobiographies or biographies adorning the shelves. You can add these to your list but remember they have been published because of who they are. Most of us will only have work published because of what we have done.

If you already know what your life-story will focus on, check to see if anything else has been written on that subject. One life-story, *Call the Midwife by Jennifer Worth*, is set in 1950's East End of London and tells the tale of a midwife and the women she encounters. This story has been so popular there would be no point in writing a similar tale. However, if you were a midwife in the 1960's in Scotland, that would be an entirely different story and something readers would find interesting and informative. When you have decided on your theme or focus, read other people's stories to make sure yours is different, unusual and just what an editor would want.

Read for pleasure but also read with a critical eye. Look at autobiographies that are in print to see how long they are, how many chapters they have and what kind of style they are written in. Ask yourself where does the story start, where does it end and what makes it a good – or bad – read.

Do the characters come alive for you? Can you see the places that are being described? Does the writing make you feel happy, sad or emotional? These are all good questions to ask of any life-story that you read. If you look at other people's work critically, you can learn what works and what doesn't, picking up tips for when you begin to write your own stories.

Everyone has a Story to Tell

Don't worry if at this stage if you think your life hasn't been exciting enough or that you don't know anybody who you could write about. Everybody has life stories to tell and everybody's life is worth putting on paper.

Start to think about the elements that have made up your life or that of another person or organization. What are the main events that have occurred? Will they be of interest to family members or the general public?

Decide on what type of writing you would like to start with and how you would like to see it produced and you will have started to think like a life-story writer. The world of telling life's tales beckons.

Chapter Two

Getting Started

Becoming a Writer

Writers come in all shapes, sizes, ages and are from all backgrounds – in fact that is the beauty of being a writer, anyone can do it if they so desire. There is no perfect writer and no particular type of person that makes a brilliant writer. Some say getting published is just luck, others say its destiny. Or it could just be hard work and perseverance!

People do not become best-selling authors overnight. Yes, there are some surprise book publications that turn a writer into an overnight celebrity but most writers spend years writing, perfecting their craft, enduring rejection and also having successes.

The life of a life-story writer is no different. If you want your work to be published, it has to be legible, have a good plot and contain characters that your readers, whether they're your family or the general public, will be interested in.

But before we get started on the nuts and bolts of life-story writing, you will want to organize your time, space and resources. Preparing yourself will make you feel like a writer. Knowing when and where you are going to write will give you the impetus you need to really get started as a life-story writer.

Your Writing Space

Organizing your writing space is an important part of being a writer. Try to find a space in your house where you can study and write comfortably. You'll need a few shelves and a desktop to call your own. If you don't have a specific room to study in, think about using up a corner of your bedroom, the gap under the stairs or that awkward alcove.

There is no need at this stage to fit your space with the latest in office equipment but it is worth thinking ahead. While pen and paper is all you'll need to begin with, you will need access to either a typewriter or computer. Editors will only accept typed submissions whether sent as hard copy or email. Handwritten life stories are never accepted and may never even be read.

You don't have to rush out and buy a computer straight away. Libraries, Internet cafes and community centers often have computers that can be used for a minimal fee and if you really can't bear the thought of typing, there are professional services that will do this for you. However, you will find it much easier and less costly if you use your own computer or laptop in the long run.

Aim to have a space that you can collect your research in: that has room for folders, boxes and files. You will be surprised at how many documents, printed sheets and family mementos you will end up gathering. Having a notice-board or wall space can also help by having reminders of what you are working on, like your timeline or plot, easily visible. Keeping your space organized and tidy will be of benefit when it comes to locating important research and your writing materials.

What You Will Need

Once you have your space sorted, you will need some basics such as:

- Pens and paper
- Notebooks
- A dictionary for correct spelling
- A thesaurus for alternative word use
- Paperclips (editors hate staples!)
- A large envelope or folder for cuttings
- Box files or large folders for storing your research

You will add to your office area as times goes on. A computer or laptop will be essential for typing your work. A printer will see all your writing come to life and a shredder can help compact documents you don't need.

It is essential to be well-organized once you are writing and especially if you are sending multiple stories out to editors and publishers. In order to keep track of your work, you can use a ledger, card file system or computer spreadsheet to make a note of what you send, where, when and to whom. When you receive a reply about your work, you can make a note of it. Hopefully, it will be an offer of publication and you can note details like whether photographs are needed or the amount of payment you will receive. If the reply is negative, you can send your work out again making a note of the new market details.

You will also need to check facts from regularly. Just because you are writing life stories does not mean that your story won't contain any facts. Think of stories that are set in a specific historical period or contain a true-life event. They are packed with facts so elements of a life-story must be checked for accuracy.

Reference books like encyclopedias are handy to have on the shelf. Look in charity shops or second-hand bookshops for inexpensive reference guides. Pick up books and other printed material on subjects that interest you or will feature in your writing. You will build up your own reference library as you progress as a writer.

Time and Commitment

So you have your writing space, now you need to organize your time. Aim to find some quiet time for your research and writing. This is easier said than done if you have children, grandchildren, a hectic job or live in shared accommodation but try to manage what time you have to maximum efficiency.

Attempt finding a time when you won't be disturbed. This

could be early in the morning before anyone else is up, in your lunch hour or after the children are in bed. Pick a time that should remain relatively interruption free. Announce to your family that it is your writing time and shut yourself away. Switch off your phone and refuse to answer the door!

Tell yourself that this is your writing time and it is not for anything else. You need to commit to the time you have allotted. It is so easy to sit down and then think of a hundred and one chores you should do or errands you should run. This is a way of putting off your writing time and many writers fall foul to it. Work out a schedule and stick to it.

Places like libraries and cafes can be good writing areas if you really can't find a quiet moment at home. Some writers enjoy watching the world go by as they work on their stories but it can also be a distraction too.

If you have days where you just can't find the time for writing then use spare moments to think about what you will write. Use long car journeys to mull over your life-story ideas, think about your writing while in the bath, come up with notions for describing your characters while waiting for the bus. Use the time you have spare in your day to think as a writer as well as write like one.

Finding Ideas

You might think that you already have the idea for your life-story. If it's about you, what other ideas could you possibly want? In the next chapter, we will look at where to start your stories and how to consider themes. Writing a story, whether for a magazine or a book, will need structure. It will need good characters and might be placed in a historical context. So you will need to start thinking of ideas for your writing like shall I write a piece about my surgery for a health magazine? Could I use the theme of working as a bus driver for a book? Would my family be interested in reading about my years living on a French vineyard?

You might also want to consider ideas for writing other people's stories. What about a tale of when Granddad fought in the Second World War? Or when Great Aunt Ada was a suffragette? Not to mention, Uncle Pete's time on an oil rig? When you start thinking about your life and others, there are lots of ideas that will surface. Not only will you come up with the main idea but when you focus in on a story, you will need to start taking notes and working out how exactly that story will be told.

Ideas will come to you at the strangest times so don't forget to have a notebook handy at all times. Leave one by your bedside, one in the front room and carry a small-sized one in your bag or the car for whenever you travel. Some writers use digital recorders so that they can easily record thoughts as they come to them and play them back later when they are sitting at their desk. If you are on the go a lot, this may be an option for you as they are small enough to fit into your bag or pocket. They can also be of use when you are visiting locations.

Say you visit a war memorial whilst writing your Granddad's story, you can read out any information or notices that are on display and record them for use at a later date. You will also find yourself talking to your family and friends as you investigate your or their story. A digital recorder can be used to store up your conversations but do remember to tell people they are being recorded. Taking notes or recordings of times, events, places and people will give you great ideas to use in your writing and facts to look up when you are doing your research.

Jot down your thoughts when you are able to, asking yourself questions based on the five W's: who, why, what, where and when. Have you got the basis for a story? Would other people be interested to read what happened next? Keep a notebook with you for occasions like this. It's surprising how often you will think of something and if it's not written down, will forget it as easily!

Whilst you are working on your ideas, also check out magazines, journals or publishers that might be interested in your writing and make a note of them. Look at magazines that you would like to write for and think about what type of life-story or article they might be interested in. Use your notebook to jot down your ideas, the magazine contact details and any guidelines they may have.

And there you will have started writing. They may only be notes to start with but once the idea is there you can build on it. Remember one scribble in a notepad could turn into a published life-story.

Using your Memory

Your life writing depends on your memory and your ability to recall past events. But how good is your memory? If five different family members were all at a wedding, they would each remember it in a different way. One might remember the dresses more, another the food, another the cars the wedding party arrive in – memory is selective and it links to what each person sees as important or relevant.

When we recall memories we think of them as a narrative; as a story that we relive. This story can get stuck in our minds and might even have been put there by other people's recollections. Childhood memories can often be planted by the memories of your parents or grandparents. This can be supported by photographs that confirm an event but do you really remember it?

People recall memories from different perspectives and this is something you should be aware of when writing life stories. If you are writing about an ancestor, talk to the people who knew them and you will find lots of differing stories come to light. Even if you are only finding out about them from letters or family diaries, you will see how people differ in their views of other people, events and occasions. Be aware of differing perspectives and use it to jog your own memory when looking at your recollections from different angles.

One way to check your reminiscences is to ask yourself questions outside of the immediate memory. Think of your first day at school. I remember being stung on the head by a bee and not much else. But wait – what was I doing at the time? I think I was playing Lego. Who comforted me? My nursery school teacher but what was her name? I think I remember my Nan coming to collect me and the teacher telling her why I was so upset. But what was the color of the room? Who were my friends? What did the school look like? Ask yourself questions like this to try and tease out more of your memories. You have memories that have been buried away but that you do still remember if you delve a little deeper.

Memories can also come to you through association and you should jot these down if they occur. Associative memories are the ones that strike you when you hear a certain song, visit a place you have been to before or smell a scent like home-cooking. Our bodies use our senses to store moments in our lives and these can come back to us at the strangest times.

Try playing some music from different times in your life. What do you remember of when you first heard those songs? Can you recall parties or family occasions that they were played at? A song that you and your partner felt was just for you? Or something that was always on the radio at work?

Memories come back to us but they are not entirely trust-worthy and can change over time. The older we get, the more we have to remember so recall becomes more difficult and more open to question. Sometimes our imagination helps out by filling in the gaps but sometimes we will need to check if our memories are correct by looking at family documents and talking to family and friends.

Up in the Attic

One place to start checking your memory is your home! Dig out all those old photos, diaries and family documents. Have you saved things like ticket stubs or programmes from events and occasions? Have you kept mementos from holidays and events in your life? All those things will jog your memory and hopefully give you concrete dates and facts.

When researching the finer points of your life and others, have a look at what evidence you have up in the attic, in the basement or in the bottom drawer, any place where you save the odd bits of paper and mementos that we all seem to collect over the years. If you can, check out your family's drawers and boxes. You might turn up some surprises!

In particular, look for certificates (births, deaths, marriages), photographs, passports, wills, military records, medals and badges, school exam results or certificates, home movies, family bibles and prayer books, newspaper cuttings that have been saved, letters or postcards, diaries and recipe books.

You could use a cork notice board to pin some of these things on and have it by your writing area. This can be helpful as a memory board and you can add to it or take mementos away as you use them in your writing. (Be sure to use copies if you do not want to mark your original material.)

Moving Forward

Once you have an idea and you've looked for supporting documents, you need to start writing. Gene Fowler said 'Writing is easy. All you have to do is stare at a blank piece of paper until drops of blood form on your forehead.' We hope that doesn't happen to you! But it does alert us to the fact that writing doesn't always come easy.

You may be writing at the moment or having trouble getting started. You might need more time for your writing or are in need of a burst of creativity. How can you move forward and keep going on the path of a life-story writer?

One of the best ways is to talk to like-minded people. You could join a writing group or one of the many forums for writers on the Internet. Here you can swop tips and ask for advice and information. If you don't have a local writing group, think about starting one yourself. There may be other people in your locality that are interested in writing and you can be a support for each other.

As we discussed in chapter one, reading other people's work can be beneficial. It's also a good idea to buy writing magazines that will give you tips on all forms or writing and let you know if there are competitions or markets that you could send your work to. Book-trade publications will also show the current market trends and what new books are due out soon.

Your Daily Routine

Consider all the things that you can do that add to your identity as a writer. Small actions on a daily basis will help you to feel you are moving forward. What habits or practices would support you in becoming a writer? What action, if taken on a regular basis, would make a difference to you and support your writing?

Remember the small things that nourish you and provide you with satisfaction, such as taking a walk, listening to a CD, talking to a friend or reading a good book. List small actions you can add into your daily routine that will support your writing, giving you time to think, jot down ideas or investigate some family history further. Are there things there already that support your writing like reading the morning newspaper or catching up on a good book before you fall asleep?

The Action Plan

See where you have 5, 10, 15 minutes to spare. These are going to be times when you do something related to writing. Sit down and work out your writing schedule. You don't have to commit to this every day – we all know how life contrives to get in the way! But even if you can't have a serious, sit down all day at the computer writing day, you can schedule in small actions that will make you feel like you are progressing. Write your list, noting your quiet times and how you can use them to be a writer. The more you add in, the more you will feel like a writer, whether you are churning out 5,000 words a day or not.

Chapter Three

The Time of Your Life

Where to Start

You don't need to start at the beginning and end at the end. You might like to but you don't have to. Writing from your birth to your old age might be of interest to your family but publishers will expect something different. Think of the autobiographies that focus on certain times or events in people's lives. They don't run in a straight line from birth to old age. In fact, many of the writers aren't even old!

A good book starts where there is action. It jumps you straight into a momentous event that is happening to the main character. In a life-story, you or the person you are writing about, are the main character and part of your research is to decide where and when the most exciting events take place.

Stop for a minute and think of the five most important events in your own life. They could be getting married, having children, getting a brilliant job, starting college and losing a loved one. We all share similar occasions within our life cycles even though they change with the culture and society we live in.

Pick one event – let's say getting that job – and think about how you could start writing at that point in your life. Wouldn't it be more interesting for the person who is reading your writing to share your feelings about the first day there and the work thereafter rather than wade through pages of days where you looked for a job, went for interviews, waited for the phone to ring?

The examples of marriage, children, work and bereavement have been written about over and over again, and the experience is different in every person's life, but if you are considering having your work published, you need to concentrate on the most unusual, different, exciting and disturbing events. Readers need to feel that they are learning something new and reading something different. They need to feel in touch with the main character so that they want to continue reading about them. Your role is to create a story that they won't put down after the first page.

Think about where the action in a life-story is and what the most momentous events were. All the above elements are in my life-story but so too is working with a circus, leaving home at fifteen, travelling in Africa, getting arrested and building my own home. These events are more likely to interest readers than the same old life events that everyone goes through. And your family would much rather know your secrets too!

The Main Events

To truly realize the main events, you are going to have to think out your life-story or the story you are writing for someone else. In order to do this, you may need to start at the beginning. I know I just said that books don't have to start that way, and they don't, but your planning and research should. You won't necessarily use all the information you find in your research but it will help you to understand your main character, whether it's yourself, or an ancestor.

Imagine you are writing about your grandfather. In order to understand his life, know where he went and what he did, you will get a better picture by looking at his life from A to B. Looking at your own life in this way will also help you to pick out the main events and perhaps even concentrate on one main aspect.

There is a difference between what our society tells us are the key events in our lives and how we actually feel about them. Graduation is a key event but what if you didn't graduate or you didn't get the marks you needed to get into a certain university? What if you did get married but realized as the ceremony progressed that this wasn't the person you wanted to spend the rest of your life with? The main events in our lives may not be as inspiring or exciting as they are meant to be.

Other things that have happened to us may have more importance. It could be something you have learned, something you were involved in or something that happened to you that was totally unexpected. The same goes for members of your family. What are the most important times in your life and theirs?

Childhood

Let's look at what could be different here. Everyone is born. That's stating the obvious but look at all the different ways in which that can happen from highly surgical births to home births surrounded by family. Look at the times in which you were born. What was happening in the world at large? What were the customs and practices surrounding your birth?

What kind of family were you born into? Rich or poor? Old-fashioned or modern? Was the birth celebrated or not? The further you delve into birth stories, the most information you will get.

If you are researching an ancestor that was born in the 1800's or 1900's for instance, you could find out what births were like then. What were the medical practices, if any, at the time? What was the rate of child mortality? How were babies dressed and how were they fed? Childhood has been written about in some amazing autobiographies. The further back into history we go, the more unusual and different upbringings appear to us. So much happens in childhood: psychologically, emotionally, physically and developmentally. Childhood is about growing up and growing into the adult you are going to be. When looking at any life-story including childhood, consider the following elements:

- The birth
- Childhood health, diseases and illnesses

- The relationship to parents, siblings and other relatives
- Friend and playmates
- Enemies or people that made life miserable
- Food – likes and dislikes, what was popular at the time
- The Family Home
- Holidays
- Childhood achievements
- Toys, books, games and entertainment
- School and education

The Teenage Years

Everybody had them although they might want to forget them! Out of all the stages of child development, the teenage years are the most disruptive, challenging and emotionally charged. For some of us, they passed in a blur of parties, school life and parental constraint. For others, it meant leaving home, finding a first love or getting a first job. Because there are many firsts within the teenage years, they can hold very vivid memories.

This time of life is about identity and what does a teenager use to build on or confirm their identity? Trends, music, fashion, hairstyles, a social life, movies and friends – they are all part of a teenager's world. So to, is the influence that teachers, parents, peers and carers exert on teenage lives.

All these examples can be used when writing about teenage life. Examine the roles that they play to flesh out your story. Don't forget to consider the emotions, thoughts and feelings that run through a teenager's head. What concerned you? What did you worry about? It could be anything from personal struggles like fitting in and looking good to global concerns like climate change or the threat of war.

School

School, of course, is a factor, whether there was a good education, a home education or a complete lack of education!

The school environment includes subjects, exams, achievements or disappointments, extracurricular activities like sports and educational day-trips. Teachers, friends and enemies populate the school world. Bullying may have been a factor or flirtations with the opposite sex.

When we look back in history, there was a marked difference in the education of girls and boys. Religious orders may have controlled local schooling. Different sexes were often segregated. Travel to school could have been over many miles. The leaving age was lower and children went out to work much sooner.

Whatever time you are looking at when you are writing life stories, school and education can be an interesting subject and it fits neatly into writing about childhood or the teenage years.

Love

Love, or the lack of it, has been the theme of many an autobiography or biography. Some of the latest books deal with divorce, coming out or sensational love affairs. Love is something that you might feel very strongly about. If you have had an amazing relationship, you might want to tell the world about it but it does need to be amazing to sell.

Although you may have been married for forty years, it may not be enough for a book of some length. Look more closely at what made your relationship so special and what its main events were.

More than any other subject, love needs a theme behind it to make it out of the ordinary. How about a tale of love against all the odds, revenge against an ex-lover, a long-lost love now found? Consider that love doesn't have to be about a couple or sexual exploits. It could be the love between a mother and her son, an unbreakable family bond between siblings or the love for an adopted child who wants to find their real parents.

Work

This area of life writing is becoming more and more popular. If you, or an ancestor, have had a really amazing job – like a spy, astronaut or archaeologist – you have the basis for a life-story that people would be fascinated to read about. But it's not just the amazing jobs that sell copies. Many books cover jobs that we would see as ordinary but the historical background, description and stories of people within the story make them great reads.

Looking in my local library, I found books written by midwives, bus conductors, cooks, nurses, servants and miners. Jobs that we might think are ordinary but essential. What they all have in common is that they bring alive a certain time and place. We have fixed ideas about some occupations and these books help us to change our assumptions and really see an area of work from a key person's perspective.

Considering Themes

When you have looked at the main events in your life or another person's, ask yourself if there is a reoccurring theme. A theme is something that stands out, a subject or pervading idea that continues through the life-story you are writing about.

It can also be the story behind the story. Say you write about your three marriages, aren't you really saying something about perseverance? Or you write about your families exploits as refugees – it could be triumph over adversity.

If your story has a theme, you can concentrate on the events and occasions, the thoughts and the feelings, that support this. Is your story a tale of love lost, perseverance or redemption? What about gratitude, challenges, or revenge? Having a theme gives your writing meaning and purpose and helps the reader to understand what has motivated this time in your life. There are many themes you can choose from and it might take an amount of writing before you see one appearing in your work. Look out for it as you continue writing. Here are some other themes that might appear – betrayal, obsession, bitterness, courage, discovery, friendship, rescue, sacrifice, shame, temptation and victory. An exercise that might help you discovery your theme is to think about what might be written on the back of your book. You know the blurb that you read first to see if the book will interest you? Something like 'This is a tale of betrayal, lost love and the ultimate revenge'. What is your tale about?

Special Areas of Expertise

Did one of your ancestors invent a product that we all use today? Was your great great grandfather a Native American shaman? Did you spend fifteen years teaching the children of a tribe in the Congo?

All of these are examples of the way in which some people show an area of expertise in their lives. It could be through work, travel or a life-long hobby or interest but if there has been a build up of years that shout experience, expertise and enthusiasm then you have material for a life-story.

Hobbies can be overlooked as things that people do to fill their time but individuals build up great knowledge from what they do in spare moments. Like the gardener who propagates a new variety of plant or who stores a huge global collection of seeds. Or the man who collects vintage machinery, restores it and takes his collection to agricultural shows around the country. These can be undiscovered gems that will make for fascinating life stories.

Travel

This type of life-story is slightly different to the others. It has more structure and will tell of a particular trip taken at a particular time. It has readymade dates and an itinerary although what might have happened on the trip could be totally unexpected. It could be a road trip or motor-home journey that took in amazing places and people.

Travel can also be a journey with a purpose like taking

supplies to Third World countries or a trip to research dialects in different regions. Some popular travel life stories have been about a move to a new home in a different country. Not only will life stories be interesting to read but they will also be informative for people who are considering it themselves.

Or it could be a holiday that you or the person you are writing about took that had disastrous or comedic consequences. Think back to all your holidays, including childhood ones, to see if there is one in particular worth writing about.

Skeletons in the Cupboard

Unfortunately, life is not always good to us. People have told tales of the times in their lives when they experienced, abuse, trauma, neglect and worse. This type of writing can be extremely therapeutic but can also open up old wounds. When you write about a time that was traumatic, you relive it and this can cause mental and emotional upset. If you want to tell the world what happened to you then do get support from a therapist or counselor. I cannot emphasize this enough. Don't let the writing of a book bring you so much pain that you can't deal with it. Plan your supports in advance so you have qualified people to talk to if you need them.

We also have to take into account the effect the story will have on its readers, especially your most nearest and dearest. If this is a true skeleton in the cupboard that your family have no idea about, you might want to break it to them first or let them read your writing before it ever gets anywhere near a publisher or editor.

There is another side to this which has legal implications. If you are writing about serious harm that befell you and are naming names, you need a solicitor's advice. Some countries have freedom of speech where anything can be printed but other countries have strict limitations on anything that is libelous or defamatory. The last thing you want if you are baring your soul is a court case. I'm not saying don't write about skeletons as your story deserves to be told. Just check out the legal implications before you try to get your work published to save yourself any further anguish.

Bringing Your Story to Life

Whatever time in your life you choose to write about, it must be brought alive for your readers. At this point, I am talking about the little everyday things that make up daily life. Before we get stuck into the nuts and bolts of writing, consider the little things that will make your writing seem real and believable. This way you can get started on your research and be prepared to add it into your writing as you go along.

Start thinking about the finer details you could include. This will also give you something creative to do when you need a break from your actual writing. Think about:

- Fashion, makeup, toiletries, clothes and hair styles
- Music, TV, radio, films
- Transport – personal and communal
- Food – meals and snacks
- Drinks – including alcoholic tipples
- Household chores – equipment, appliances, methods
- Communication – telephone, telegram, word of mouth, emails
- The Home – heating, running water, the amount of rooms
- Pets or farmyard animals
- Reading materials – books, newspapers and magazines
- Religious practices
- Social life – theatre, community groups, clubs
- The political situation

When you are writing a life-story, these things will help the reader to understand the times you are writing about. For example, if you read a story and the Beatles are playing in the local concert hall, you immediately think of the sixties. If a woman has to take her ration book to the shops with her to buy dried egg powder and flour that tells us the story is set in the Second World War. So not only do the finer details bring your story to life but they alert the reader to the time of your life and make it a more authentic experience for them.

Now start writing! Pick one of the areas we have discussed in this chapter, one that moves you to write. What topic fills you with emotion and desire to get your words on paper? Start practicing with short pieces of work by exploring the time of your life in all its finest details.

Chapter Four

Getting that Story into Shape

What do you do with all your ideas, themes, topics and research once you've collected them? It's time to work out your plot – that is the structure of your story, the framework that you will build upon and unravel. It can be used for a book-length life-story or a shorter form to be published in a magazine.

Plot

Plot contains core elements that you need to consider when writing your life-story:

- Characters
- Setting or place
- Objects or subjects
- The Event
- The Grand finale

Characters

Well, that would include you! But who else featured in your life that you will include in your life-story? Teachers, employers, spouses, children ...write a list of all the possible characters and decide, apart from yourself, who are the main ones? We will look at characterization in more detail in the next chapter.

Settings and Places

Your life-story will be set in a certain time or focus on a specific job or company or community. You need to think of the background to your story as much as the story itself. For example, if some of your story is set in California in the Swinging

Sixties – what are the sights, sounds, smells and tastes you could use to describe being there? You will need to bring your setting alive for your reader, using senses, emotions and vibrant description of locations and places. More about this in chapter six.

Where you went to work or where you were born may be vivid in your mind. They might feature in your writing but it's up to you to give a good enough description so that they can appear not only on the page but in your reader's minds too. They weren't there and might not have ever visited the place so it is your job to fill in all the finer details for them so they can relive your story with you.

Objects or Subjects

Sometimes an object can play a role in a story – a treasure chest, a family heirloom, a house, the list is endless. Are there any objects you want to include? Is there something, perhaps you were given as a child, that has had an influence on your life?

Is there a subject or theme that runs through your story? Most recent life stories have focused on abuse, midwifery, gangs, expeditions and war. Look at your life-story to see if there is a subject that runs through your writing that you could expand on.

Event

What are the main events that you are going to concentrate on? It could be one momentous event that changed your life or a series of events that happened over 20 or 30 years. Think chapters of a book. If your life-story was to be published and it had 15 chapters in it, what events would appear in each of those chapters?

Grand Finale

This is where you wrap up your story and tie up all your loose ends. Only you know what part of your life you want to end your writing on. Just make it good. Leave your readers feeling satisfied and glad they read that particular life-story. Answer any questions your readers may have and bring your writing to its natural conclusion.

Plot is your guideline to writing your life-story. You have control of it but make sure you include the five elements. Use it in note form to shape your ideas or flesh it out as a first draft. You can write as little or as much as you like when you work out your plot. It is a tool for your use and it will help to guide you through your writing. Plotting helps you to plan the forward movement of your book or story so that you never lose track of where it is going.

Subplots

Your main plot might be supported by subplots. In a short life-story, there is never much room for a subplot but in a book you have room for several, if you wish. Subplots are just sub-stories. They are smaller stories that run alongside your main plot, mixing and intersecting with it at various points. They can happen over a number of chapters or just a few.

The most common form of subplot is the story of another character. Say you are writing your life-story but you are including your relationship with a Great Aunt or work colleague, you might include their story as a subplot. A timeline will help you to tie your main plot and subplots together. Don't worry if adding subplots sounds confusing. Write your life-story the way you want to and just consider whether there is a subplot when you come to the editing stage. That way you can add to it or change it as appropriate for the entire book.

Timelines

Using a timeline is a great way of getting your story into shape and combining all your plot elements. It is an extremely helpful tool if you are still uncertain of what to write and you need to think about the stages you have gone through in your life. It will also help you to keep a track of your plot once you start writing so that nothing is forgotten and everything is included. There is a lot to plan when writing a story and especially when writing a book but it can all be pulled together by using a timeline.

The basic idea is to plot your life-story from beginning to end using dates and events so that you don't lose track of the story and always know what you are writing next. Your final book may not follow such a linear structure but at this stage, it will help to think out your timeline from A to B.

You can make it as simple as you want:

1950 Born

1954 Started nursery school

1957 Started primary school

Or more detailed:

1950, 22nd December – Born in London General Hospital. Mum, Dad and younger brother, Mike, present

1954, 4th September – Started Thornhill nursery school. Mrs. Reynolds was first teacher. Friends were Mark and Frank.

1957, 1st September – Started Meadlands primary school. Mr. Drummond was teacher. No friends at first. Bullied by John.

The idea is to note all your key dates and events in sequence and have them readily available. You can use a table printed off your computer or pin a big sheet of paper on the wall above your writing desk. If you use a cork notice board, you can add photos, tickets, postcards... anything that will jog your memory and help your creativity to flow.

It can also help if you get stuck writing your narrative or find you have gone off on a tangent. You can check back to your timeline to see where you are in the story and to make sure you haven't forgotten anything. It will bring you back to the dates and events and their sequence which means your reader won't be confused by your writing. You can check back with your timeline to see where you are in your story and to make sure you haven't forgotten anything. It ensures that your work doesn't become confusing. It will all be clear to you and ultimately your reader. A timeline can also help you to keep track if you are writing a life-story about someone else when the events and dates are not familiar to you. You can build up your research and have it in noted in a place that you can easily see. It will show you the gaps where you need to research more and the overall picture of the story as it unfolds.

A short life-story timeline will only stretch over a day or two but a book-sized life-story timeline will be much longer. A separate timeline can be made up for each chapter as well as the book as a whole. Subplots can be added to the timeline or worked out separately and indicated on the main timeline so you remember to add the subplot details into your main writing.

Planning Your Chapters

When you have worked out your timeline, you will be able to see more clearly how to divide your work into chapters if you are writing a book-length life-story. Books vary in the amount of chapters they have. It could be as little as three or as many as twenty. There is no set rule as to how many chapters you have to have.

Once you have considered your plot and timeline, you should be able to see clearly how you can divide up your life-story. Think about your main events and see if they could take a chapter each. It will help to title each chapter. You can change the title later on but for now, you can label them growing up, work, etc so they have a working title.

Once you have split your book into chapters, it can help to write a chapter by chapter synopsis. This will help you to have a plan of what each chapter contains so that if you get stuck or have a case of the dreaded writer's block, you know exactly where you are and what you have to write next. Publishers will also ask for a chapter list when considering your work for publication.

Start by making a numerical list of your chapters and their titles. Then add notes under each chapter heading of what it will contain. You don't have to write loads. Think back to the plot elements and include what characters will appear, what the events are, where the action is or the thoughts and feelings that will occur in the chapter. Use it as a framework to build upon and edit at will. As you begin writing, you may find that your chapters change; that you think something should be added later on in the book or come first.

To help you order your chapters, you can also use Post-Its or cards and use each one per chapter. Having them all spread out in front of you, you can swap them about until the framework looks right.

At this point, you might be saying, I just want to get started! If you feel like writing, write! But the more you plan and organize, the more chance you have of completing your book. By organizing your work before you start and planning out your story, you stand a good chance of seeing it through from beginning to end. Many writers run out of steam after a few hundred words but if you have worked out your timeline, know what your chapters contain, and can see how your plot moves forward then you have an excellent chance of getting that book written.

The Greater Timeline Perspective

We have looked at using a timeline to plot your story and plan your chapters. It helps to organize your writing so that it has better pace and structure. Whatever time you are writing about will sit against the greater timeline perspective or the world environment. By this, we mean what was happening in the world during the time of your story. The greater timeline perspective looks at what was occurring and what events were happening that could be good details to add into your writing. It could be something as small as the finer details we looked at like what song your character is listening to on the radio. Today, it could be Madonna but in the Seventies, it might have been The Kinks.

Or it could be more monumental like a woman having the choice to work in an ammunitions factory or join the forces rather than working at home or childminding. The greater timeline perspective gives your story a wider view. What were the important things happening in the world at the time of your story that can add to its background and setting?

You can mark out another timeline to have alongside your plot timeline or just add in notes to your original timeline. Note when to use world events to add to your creation of setting and atmosphere. What is your character's reaction when they hear Elvis has died or JFK has been shot? Key events can add valuable authenticity to your story.

Structure

A life-story has a beginning, middle and end. Think hook, unravel and tie the knot – no, not fishing or knitting! To begin, you hook, in the middle, you unravel and at the end, you tie the knot including any loose strings. This is where you get down to really writing your life-story so bear these points in mind.

Beginnings

Story beginnings are about hooking your reader in. It is said that readers will only go as far as the first two lines before deciding whether they want to read on. You have to captivate your audience, give them a taste of your life-story and make them want to find out more. Your first paragraph must be attention-grabbing so your readers, family or publisher will be intrigued to find out exactly where your story goes. Once upon a time is definitely out!

You will need to introduce yourself as the main character in your first paragraph in such a way that your reader becomes interested in following your story.

Look at the difference between these two beginnings:

I woke up at 8. Every morning I got the train and then walked from the station to work.

The incessant tringing of the alarm awoke me, signaling another day at Thatchers & Co. If I didn't get a wriggle on, I'd miss the train yet again.

In the first example, you know I am going to have an ordinary day. I'll probably read the paper, go to work, come home, eat and sleep. Not much of a story there. But in the second example, what is Thatcher's & Co? Why have they missed the train before? Is there a sense of reluctance when the alarm sounds? This paragraph makes us ask questions of our character, who within two lines, we already want to know more about. Make sure your beginning makes your readers ask similar questions and prompts them to read further to find the answers.

Middle

This is the bulk of your story where all unravels. Readers will find out more about you, where you lived, who you spent your time with and where the events of your life-story will unfold. Your writing will flow here as the story continues. Go with your creative flow but then check that the pace of your story builds as it progresses. Keep an eye on your timeline and your plot to make sure all your elements are included.

Keep your writing descriptive and let your characters tell the story for you. Show, don't tell. This is hugely important in any type of creative writing and something that beginner writers should be aware of before they even attempt to write. It is a skill to practise and also watch out for. Make sure your life-story writing is showing and not telling.

Stories are driven forward by the acts, thoughts and deeds of their characters. So in writing what a character is doing, you should show your reader not tell them. Here are some examples:

> **Telling:** Jake was unhappy.
> **Showing:** Jake wiped the tears from his eyes with an old used hankie.
> **Telling:** Kathleen was so excited.
> **Showing:** Kathleen ripped the wrapping off her birthday present.

Your reader wants to experience your story through the eyes of its characters so whatever is happening to them, the reader wants to be able to visualize it. Telling them does not attract them to the plight of your characters.

Showing helps your reader to experience your story as if they were there. Telling just gives them information and it can make the reading experience boring. To make sure, you are 'showing' when you write use action, dialogue and the five senses to move your story forward.

End

Your ending must satisfy your reader. It sums up the purpose behind the plot. It rounds up the events, yourself and your characters in a convincing grand finale. The majority of life stories end with a twist in the tale; an added surprise, an extra kick or special punch-line. If using this kind of ending, it has to be clever and take the reader by surprise but also make them realize that they could have seen it coming.

There are different types of endings in stories; romantic, humorous, happy, upbeat – all positive and uplifting for the reader. But life stories can also contain much tragedy and sadness. Write what you need to write at all times but bear in mind that you will have readers who will expect your ending to satisfy them.

Style and Tone

Life stories vary in style, tone and length. Style is something you will develop for yourself. It is unique to you and you might not even realize your own style until you have had more practice. It could be formal, informal, chatty or humorous.

Books and magazines have their own tone and this is based on the market that they are aiming for; the style they use for their type of readers. Magazines differ in the way their stories are written because they are aiming at a certain demographic. If you decide you would like to see some of your life stories published in a magazine, you will need to understand what readership they target and adjust your style and tone accordingly.

Books also differ in tone. Look at the life stories of David Beckham and Bill Clinton. Very different people with different careers and lives. Their books are both written in different styles because they are aimed at different types of readers. Who is your life writing aimed at?

Book Length

Many writers ask how long should their book be. There is no set figure but, in general, a fiction novel would contain around 60,000 words. If you wrote 500 words a day, five days a week, you would have a book length manuscript in six months time. This is not as scary as it sounds! Some days you will write more than others, some days less.

However, there are books of all lengths, from 30,000 – 100,000 is a good range. Your life-story can be any length but do have an idea of whether you are just writing a story or a book before you begin. Stories can be as small as 1,200 words for a one pager or 3,000 plus for a serial or story by installments. Write to the length that suits you. When you come to the editing stage, you will see whether you need to write more at certain points or have to cut out others. By then you will have a better idea of your book length.

Chapter Five

You're the Star!

Characters bring stories to life. What would a story be without the trials and tribulations of the characters it contains? In this chapter, we will be looking at you, the main character and the other characters you will include in your life stories. The term 'character' might make you think of people that are made up, people that a writer just invents for their stories purpose, but they are also the people you portray in your writing, the people that have shared your life and who you now are going to recreate on paper.

When writing a life-story, you will be the main character unless you are writing for someone else. You are the star of your own writing. You might think that makes it the easiest thing to write about but can you see yourself as a character?

There will also be other characters in your life-story; family, friends, acquaintances, and colleagues that must all take the role of bringing your story to life and moving your story forward. These people need to be believable and appeal to your readers, as much as you do.

You as the Main Character

Characters are the true storytellers and you should endeavor to write as if you, as a character, are telling the tale. As a main character, you will unravel your story through what you say and what you do. It is your actions, thoughts and speech that propel the story forward. This can be difficult when it is your own life as you know what happens next and can see the background, the conversations and the people in your own head. Your readers do not have this prior knowledge so everything that is put down on paper must help your reader to enter your world.

Writing about Yourself

When you write about yourself, you have to bring alive the world you were living in for your readers. If your readers will just be your family, they already know a lot about your attitudes, opinions and personality but that doesn't mean they know everything about you. Other readers won't know you at all so you have to make yourself as active and animated to make yourself a believable character.

You want readers to be interested in your life-story. You want your book to be the one that they choose from a bookshelf in a library or buy in a store. So you have to let them into your world by revealing your thoughts, feelings and emotions. Readers are hooked in by emotion. They want to laugh, cry and sigh along with the person they are reading about. This might mean baring your soul a bit more than usual.

Writing your own life-story can be a learning curve. You are going back to re-examine past events and as part of that, to make your readers come along with you, you have to look at what you were really feeling. Your memories of events may have dulled with time or the acceptance we gain of what has happened in our lives as we get older. To write a really good life-story, you will need to relive the key moments, places and people as they felt to you then.

When you are writing, take time to close your eyes and go back in time. Feel, with all your senses, what was happening. Then ask yourself did I really feel that? Why? Were there other emotions present at the time? And practice writing about yourself as a fully rounded character to help your readers understand what was going on in your life.

Character Biographies

Writing up a biography for yourself will help you to remember details and remind you to include basic information that your reader needs to know. You can compile a list in your notebook or on cards and include your name, physical description, age, sex, height, weight but also other characteristics like temperament, qualities, behavior, strengths, weaknesses, etc.

Fill out your biography under the following headings. Add any more you can think of.

- Name
- Address
- Age
- Sex
- Marital Status
- Children
- Height
- Weight
- Physical description
- Dress
- Pets
- Music
- Temperament
- Beliefs
- Behavioural Traits
- Likes
- Dislikes
- Relationships
- Occupation
- Hobbies
- Health
- Strengths
- Weaknesses
- Role in Story
- What is this character's purpose?
- What do they want to achieve?

As you will have changed over the course of your life, you can redo certain elements of your biography like strengths, weaknesses, likes and dislikes for the different stages in your life that you are writing about.

Other Characters

You can also do this for any other characters that appear in your life-story but especially for the main ones. All characters have personalities, character traits and personal details specific to them. You might be including an anecdote about your aunt, your grandfather or your children and you know what their personalities are like but will your reader? Not necessarily.

You should be able to answer questions about the people in your life-story. Does your character like chocolate? Would she scream if she saw a mouse? Does he watch football every Sunday afternoon? Know their actions and reactions.

It comes back to showing what your character is like as a person through the way the story is told through their eyes. They need to be as real to your readers as they have been to you so your readers will care enough to follow your story, and theirs, to the end.

You won't include all this detail in your story but in order for you to bring your characters alive you need to know them inside and out. A short story of 1,000 words has very little room for long physical descriptions or lengthy passages about your characters but a book-length story will give you more room to manoeuvre and to expand on why these people were so important in your life.

Types of Characters

A fiction novel has good and bad characters. There will always be a protagonist (the main character) and an antagonist (the bad character). These two characters create conflict and that is what can drive a plot forward. This can also work in life stories. It is doubtful that your life-story does not contain some type of antagonist whether it is an unsupportive parent, school teacher or work colleague.

Sometimes the antagonist is an obstacle or threat the main character faces rather than another person. This happens more in short stories where there is very little room for a cast of characters. A short life-story will have a primary character – who the story is about and possibly one or two secondary characters – people who interact with the primary character and that is it. A short story of 1,000 words does not have room for a cast of hundreds.

Think about the role a secondary character plays in your life-story. Did they teach you something? Help you? Support you through rough times? If you are writing about your relationship with a family member, you may take their role for granted: a mother who cared for you, a father who went out to work. But what else did they give you? A love of books, an interest in fishing or the strength and determination to be a better parent yourself – these are all examples of the added roles people play in our lives.

Checking your Characters

Your primary character is you. You are the one whose story you want to tell but be careful with secondary characters. When writing a life-story, be absolutely sure they are relevant and they have a purpose.

To check that a character is working, ask yourself

- What is their role?
- What do they contribute to the story?
- What purpose do they serve in the story?
- How do they move it forward?
- Will your reader care about them?
- If they weren't there, would they be missed?

When writing a book, you have much more freedom to have a colourful cast of characters. Some historical stories have so many characters that they have to contain a glossary of names so readers can keep up.

Concentrate on the relationship between yourself and your characters as your life-story unfolds. If your secondary characters are not moving the story forward then they are not relevant. Cut them out.

Ask questions about every person you include in your life-story. What are they doing in your story? What is their true role and purpose? They must have a purpose if they are to be included. When you are sure they have every right to be in your story, it's time to start fleshing them out. Write their biographies and examine what has made them significant in your life.

Character Grids

When you have biographies done of your secondary characters, you can check them off on a character grid. This can be done to compare the people in your life so you can see where similarities are and where differences lay. A protagonist and antagonist will have great differences but friends may have similarities.

Looking at the people in your life side by side will tell you if they are likely to work well as characters or if you are writing about conflict, whether they will work antagonistically together. On a sheet of paper, make a list of headings on the left-hand side. You can use the ones from your biographies. List things like physical appearance, dress, strengths, weaknesses, temperament, likes and dislikes. Then write down each character's details in a list next to it. You should get three or four characters on one sheet of paper, side by side. You can also do this on the computer by using a table.

This will give you an easy-to-view snapshot of their characteristics. You can display it in your writing area, perhaps with your plot, so you don't forget key details about them. Use a character grid as a memory prompt and to make sure that nothing about them is forgotten during your writing sessions.

Making your Characters Believable

Characters bring your story to life. New writers often make the mistake of writing too woodenly, as if they were giving directions or orders to their characters. The key to writing believable characters is to show what they are doing. Show, don't tell. If you tell your reader all about your characters they will get bored and feel like they are being talked down to. You need to make your characters believable by showing what they do, how they feel, and what their reactions are.

The people you include in your life-story will show their involvement in your life better through what they say and what they do. It is their actions, thoughts and speech that propel the story forward. They need to appeal to readers and make them want to read on, finding out what happens to them next and caring whether they live happily ever after or are facing a terrible fate.

Consider the characters you have read about in short stories and books. Are there any that stick out in your mind? Why do they stick out? What made you interested in them?

In order for your life-story to work, you and your supporting characters must engage your readers through emotion. A reader needs to feel sad if their character is sad, happy for them, worried about them. When they are facing a dilemma, a reader needs to care how they get through it. Care enough to read on and that's exactly what editors and publishers are looking for; characters that draw you in, make you believe in them and care about their lives for however many pages their stories last.

This goes for good and bad characters. The sun doesn't shine out of every character. Baddies need to be just as believable. A reader will look even more closely to see what happens in a bad character's life and they will hope that they have some redeeming qualities or a change of heart and attitude although this doesn't always happen. If you are including negative people in your life-story, what were the pluses of having someone like this in your life? Are there any? Did having to deal with them ultimately make you stronger or braver?

Think of Scrooge in Dickens's Christmas Carol. What an awful character is he! Yet he learns to be a better person and his life changes dramatically. A reader may begin by hating him but suspends their belief while he is visited by the ghosts of his past, present and future. They wonder – will he change his ways? At the end of the story, he has become a different man and the reader has changed their opinion of him. Although Scrooge is a work of fiction, we have many people in our lives that we have seen change and grow – some for the better, some for worse. Show their development, or lack of it, in your life-story to make them more believable characters.

Dressing your Characters

What else makes characters believable within a life-story? What about their clothes and the way they were dressed? Think of how a teenagers' fashion trends change with the times. If you are a teenager in your story and you are dressed in flares and a paisley shirt, what would that tell a reader about the times your story is set in?

Your characters need to be dressed appropriately and that goes for hair, makeup and accessories too. You might not use all the detail of their appearance in your story but some reference to their clothes will help your reader to imagine the time you are writing about.

What era would you think of if your female characters had on ball gowns and shawls? Or someone wanted to buy a dress just like Marilyn Monroe's? Clothes give readers a visual image without having to give them an exact date.

You can research clothes and costumes in many books, at

museums and online. If you are writing about your ancestors you may not be sure of the fashions that were popular or the uniforms they wore. Looking at how people dressed and what clothes they wore can be fascinating research and it will add detail to your story. It also adds authenticity to your story and makes your characters historically correct.

Viewpoint

We have looked at how to make characters work in your life story but just a word here on viewpoint. Life stories can be written in the first- or third-person viewpoint. As you are writing your own story, you will probably choose to write from a first-person perspective, eg., *I went, I spoke, I couldn't believe it when…*or first-person plural, eg., *we went, we said, we walked* if you are talking about yourself and other people.

Third-person viewpoint, eg., *he said, she went, they spoke…*, can also be used if you want to write from an outside perspective. Talking about yourself in the third person is tricky and you should only use it if you feel comfortable with it. It is more likely to be used if you are writing about a family member, an organization or business.

Don't change viewpoints in a life-story. This can work well in fiction novels where the narrative switches between characters and gives us the story from different perspectives. However, in a life-story, it will only confuse readers about who is the main character. Remember you're the star and you want your readers to know that too.

A Word of Caution

In a previous chapter, we talked about writing that could have legal implications. The same goes for writing libelous or derogatory information about characters who are real people. Nobody wants to read a book and find themselves criticized or shamed in it.

Be careful what you write if you don't want to offend anyone. Tell the people in your life that they are being included in your life-story. Let them look at something you've written about them before sending it to an editor or publisher so that you are know they are okay with it.

On the other hand, if writing your life-story, means telling the truth about what someone has done to you, you cannot help but upset people. Stories of trauma sometimes have name changes or character traits are written about so differently from the person in real life that they cannot recognize themselves.

If court cases were involved in your life-story or there are protection issues around the events you are writing about, research how much you can write about without risking prosecution. Every country has different laws so check out the legal implications in your country before you seek publication.

Chapter Six

Key Elements of Writing

In order to make your life stories genuine and authentic for your reader, there are some key elements of writing that you can use. Settings, description, dialogue and narration all build your life writing into a readable story. Techniques like creating intrigue and flash backs can liven up your plot and help to make your life-story one that readers will not be able to put down.

Settings

The setting of your life-story will reveal much to your readers. As the story progresses the settings will change or you may go back to settings you have used before. A setting is the where and when of your story. Where is the story located and at what time? Time in this sense can be the year or historical time, the time of day or the seasonal time.

Your settings should aim to make the reader familiar with the times you are writing about. If someone is having breakfast while watching the snow fall outside their window, we know that it is a winter's morning. Likewise if they are eating Ben and Jerry's ice cream in the heat of the midday sun, we know that it is summer.

If the breakfast is gruel and the ice cream is a Good Humour bar, we know that we are not in modern times. Even the smallest of details can give readers clues to where and when your story is located.

Setting can also contain elements like architecture, geography, the weather, and social and political indicators. Your setting will come alive to your readers through the details you use to describe it.

It can also bring your characters to life by showing how they live and what their surroundings are like. If their front room is full of books and papers, it can tell us that the character is studious, academic or has a love of literature. If every shelf is cluttered with photos and ornaments, trophies and certificates, it shows a person who is very proud of their family and has all their achievements on display.

The settings that are personal to your characters can tell us much about them. Are there a lot of pills on their bedside cabinet? Is their dressing table covered in makeup, lotions and potions or is the room bare, devoid of personal belongings as if they hardly live there at all? The use of well-described settings can take your readers into another world, your world and make them feel like they are really there.

Description

Settings are shown through description. For a life-story to ring true, good description is needed. There doesn't have to be pages of it or lists of how everything looked but there does need to be enough for your readers to see what you have seen and feel what you have felt.

Description provides the mood of a story. The way in which a place is described, for instance, can make us feel disgust, excitement, fear, happiness and a range of other emotions.

The sidewalk was strewn with used needles, rotting vegetables and bits of tissue that floated through the grime. Not such a nice place, is it? *The smell of candyfloss and hot dogs hit me before I had even seen the lights.* Is there a hint of excitement? Is the next scene going to be in a fairground?

You can use your description to give hints of what is to come without spelling it out. Readers do have good imaginations and while they need to know time and place, they can also fill in some of the blanks for themselves.

The golden rule about description is to make sure it is meaningful. You don't need to describe in detail Granny's bedroom unless there is a scene in your book that is situated there and even then the reader does not need to know what is in Granny's drawers! You don't need to describe a house from top to bottom if you are only walking past it in your story but if you are entering it for the first time, you might want to give us some details. Include description that is relevant, that tells your reader something new about yourself or your characters, that brings alive the story that you are telling.

Make your writing more exciting by using verbs that gives us those details. Instead of writing something like *I walked to the factory gates,* try *I stumbled through the factory gates.* Immediately your reader will be wondering why you are stumbling – could you be drunk? Hurt in some way? Or what about *I looked at the house*? Does it give a different feel if you observed it, peeked at it, glared at it or stared at it?

Use of more descriptive verbs will add color to your writing. A thesaurus can help you to find alternatives to the first word that springs to mind so that you can choose something more descriptive to bring your settings to life.

Using Your Senses

The best way of describing places, events and people in your life writing is through the use of your senses. And as we have said before what your senses felt at the time. Your readers are seeing through your eyes, hearing through your ears and feeling with your touch.

When you are recalling events, remember to ask yourself what your senses were taking in. Sight, sound, touch, taste and smell will all add to your descriptions. Try to describe your senses with more illuminating words. The sky isn't just gray, it tastes like there is thunder in the air. Granny's cooking was divine, but what did her cooking smell like as she labored all day over a hot stove?

Think outside of the box when writing descriptive passages based on your senses. We have all read descriptions that have nothing new in them like the grass was green, the trees swayed in the wind, the rain made everything wet – these are obvious and have been used over and over again. How could you describe what your senses took in differently? Make your descriptions more lively, unusual and not so run-of-the-mill and you will be giving your readers a treat.

Narration

We have already looked at viewpoint but a writer can write his or her life-story from differing perspectives of narrative voice. This shows the position of the narrator in relation to the story. Different types of narrative voice include

- Narrating from a far distance – the narrator's voice comes across as being distant and emotionally uninvolved or disinterested in the story
- Narrating from a close distance – the narrative voice is involved and passionate about the story being told
- Narrating with sympathy – here the voice of the author comes across as being empathetic with the trials of the characters
- Narrating from a standpoint – this can include overtones of an author's religious, political and sexual orientations

You can probably think of other ways in which a narrator's voice comes across in a story. When reading a book or short story, look out for the point of view that the author has taken. Be aware of the way in which you want your voice to come across in your life-story writing. You probably don't want it to seem like you are writing from a distance, a life-story is a much more involved and personal piece of writing than other forms of literature but you might want to consider whether there is an standpoint or perspective that you are writing from. If you don't spot it first, your readers surely will.

Dialogue

There are three types of speech that are used in creative writing; direct, indirect and interior. Direct speech is the type that is written into a dialogue complete with speech marks. Indirect speech reports what someone has said. For instance, *Alf told me that Peter wanted to join the army.* Interior speech tells the reader of a character's thoughts. For example, *I hate that man so much, Julia thought.*

Direct speech can cause problems for beginner writers but perfection comes with practice. Dialogue is the speech contained within a story. It is what your characters say to each other and in the case of life writing, what conversations you have had with other people, that you wish to record. Speech has meaning and is there for a purpose. It moves the story forward and breaks up the main body of text. It gives the reader a real sense of what you and your characters are really like.

Your dialogue must sound believable and be correctly presented within your life-story. Dialogue then should read as it sounds. The best way to check this is to read your dialogue aloud. Take these two lines of speech –

'I did not want the children to overhear us.'
'I didn't want the kids to hear.'

Which sounds more real? When we speak we abbreviate words, use slang and add exclamation and emphasis to certain parts so it makes sense that when we are writing dialogue, it follows our speech patterns.

Dialogue needs to be kept real. Your setting and your characters will determine what speech is used. If you were writing a life-story set in Victorian England you would use a very different type of speech to a story that's set in inner city Dublin. Try to show your story's time and place through your dialogue but don't get caught up in reproducing accents that will be difficult for people to read.

Think of how your characters really speak. A teenager would have an informal, chatty speech pattern. An upper-class person has a more formal and educated tone. Consider your characters age and background and how it has affected the way in which they talk.

Listen to dialogue on the television or radio. Note how it changes for different characters. Write your own dialogue and read it aloud. Use family and friends to take parts in written conservations so you hear whether your dialogue sounds right for your life-story. Give your characters the voice that fits them and is believable to your readers. Not forgetting your own voice too!

Dialect

Be careful with dialect and accents. Yes, your dialogue should sound real but dialect can be very difficult to read. Think of a thick Scottish accent or a London Cockney accent. If you tried to write that down in speech, for one, it would be a task in itself and for another, your readers will probably get fed up trying to work out what you are trying to say and put your book down.

You can signify how a character speaks in other ways. If you let your readers know they are from Scotland or from London in your description of them, they can imagine their type of speech without you having to write it into some form of dialect.

Or you can add in a word or two that lets the reader know where the person is from but the dialogue doesn't get swamped with strange spellings. For instance, a Scottish person would say 'aye' instead or yes or 'nae' instead of no. A Cockney speaker often punctuates their speech with 'mate' or 'guv' and this can be added in for effect. Wherever your character is from, show your readers with short phrases or sayings rather than bogging your writing down with dialect that is difficult to read.

Presentation of Dialogue

Presentation of dialogue within your life-story is important.

- Indent a new line of speech for each new speaker.
- Always use speech marks. They can be single ' or double "
  but must remain constant throughout.

    'I couldn't go out Friday night,' Jane moaned. (single)

    "I couldn't go out Friday night," Jane moaned.(double)

- Commas always stay within the speech marks.
- Punctuation marks always come within speech marks
  whether they are full stops, question marks or exclamation
  marks.
- Exclamation and question marks do not need full stops or
  commas after them.

    'Do you want a biscuit?' I asked Ryan.

    'Go away!' I yelled.

- Be wary of the he said/ she said syndrome. Your character
  can yell, scream, choke, laugh, mutter, cough, wheeze, and
  so on.

    'It's time for bed!' I called out to the children.

    'We're finished,' I screamed.

Look at the way dialogue is presented in a book and follow suit
in your own writing. If you would like more information on
grammar and punctuation, there are many good English-usage
books on the market that will refresh your memory.

Creating Intrigue

Intrigue can be described as arousing interest, curiosity, or fasci-
nation. For a reader to feel engaged in a life-story, there has to be
some intrigue, a reason why the reader keeps on reading. The
reader has to be interested in a character or curious about how
the story will turn out. They have to be fascinated as to why a
character behaves in a certain way or dying to know how they got

into their predicament – and how they will get out of it!

The key to creating intrigue is to drop hints during your telling of a story that will lead to a satisfying conclusion. You don't want to tell your readers the ending of your story but give them clues and hints as you go along so that they can pick up on the secrets of your plot. It's showing again, instead of telling.

Intrigue is created by giving your readers some information but not all. Such as *I opened the envelope with trepidation. My fingers trembled and I could feel beads of sweat forming on my brow.* This passage creates intrigue because it makes a reader ask questions of the story. What is in the envelope? Why is the character so worried about it? They don't know the answers and at the moment, can only guess. As the story develops they will get their answers, maybe in the next paragraph or not until the very end.

Intrigue creates a sense of mystery. It can be misleading, making a reader think in one direction when really the opposite is true or it can be more straightforward, building up a story with facts and clues, but not giving the game away. You don't want your writing to read like a movie you already know the ending of so use intrigue to build up curiosity in your plot.

When you are working on your plot and timeline, you can make a note of where you will add intrigue into your writing but adding hints and clues. Keep a track of where and when your writing uses intrigue and use it to build up to an incredible ending.

Flash Forwards and Flash Backs

These are two techniques that can be used in longer stories or novels. Flashing back is the most common technique and it lets your reader know something that has happened in the past. Flashing forward will give your reader a glimpse of what occurred in the future.

Although flash forwards, or prolepses, are not used as much as flash backs, they can work well in first-person narratives.

They are often used to show someone who has aged or is older or something that is happening at a future event. This technique can be used to give the reader an understanding of what happens to the characters in the future and it can be expected, imagined or anticipated.

Flash backs, also known as analepses, are the opposite and take us back in time. This technique is generally used for filling in information about a character's past. It can give us information about an event that occurred that will impact on the current story. This is quite often used to build up mystery and intrigue and to show what has happened. It also gives readers a clue about what might be the resolution of the current situation.

Writing techniques can be used to give your writing more depth but do not get too concerned about whether you are able to use them in your story. The last thing you want is to give up on your writing because you haven't been able to add in a flash back or mood change. As you write more, these things will come naturally to you but do not let yourself worry yourself out of writing!

Choosing a Good Title

Every life-story needs a good title. It's not good enough to just call it *My Story* or *A Year in the Life of...* A title should be catchy. It's the first thing a reader, editor or publisher will see of your work. You can have fun coming up with different titles and it can provide a break from the serious work of writing. Titles are something you can practice doing while you are coming up with ideas or researching your background information. At these quieter times, you might find title ideas come to you more easily. Keep a page in your notebook that is just for noting your titles.

A title needs to be short and snappy – just enough to gain attention. It also needs to give a feel for the story and this is difficult to do in so few words. Practice coming up with great titles. Play around with words, familiar sayings and catch-phrases. Three or four words are often all that are needed, especially for a short life-story. Never stretch a title to more than one sentence.

Look at titles in magazines and on books for more examples to see how those writers have encapsulated the sense of their story in so few words. Many writers use a working title whilst they are concentrating on their life-story and then go back to it once they have finished, making sure it is still appropriate for their story.

Remember once you have completed your story or novel to double-check your title to make sure it is still relevant and sounds as catchy as you can make it. You want it to shout out, pick me, pick me!

Chapter Seven

Checking the Facts

Whether you are undertaking research for your own life-story, someone else's or you are investigating a company or organization, you will need to check your facts. All life stories contain facts whether they are dates, historical events, background information or the names of people and places.

If you don't get your facts right, it will undermine your credibility as a writer and the authenticity of your work. There will always be someone who points out your mistakes so this chapter focuses on how to do your research, check your facts and ensure that your writing is as accurate as it can possibly be.

Finding Facts

Some writers find research boring. This is probably because they swamp themselves with facts, figures and data that they can see no end to. The trick with checking your facts is to research only what is absolutely necessary for your writing. It is so easy to go off on a tangent and to end up doing more research than you do writing. Staying focused is the key.

You might wonder why research is necessary for your life-story when you know what happened in it. It is invaluable for checking facts and making sure that memories are correct but research will also bring your story to life and make it much more appealing to your readers.

The research you need to do depends on what you are writing. Can you really remember the place you grew up in? Are you certain of your family tree? Can you recall what song was number one when you got married?

Research helps by building the background to your life-story and situating it in a time and place readers can recognize. For instance, if your story centers around your life in the 1960s, what were you wearing? What was in the news? What films were on at the cinema?

You can use this information to flesh out your writing so instead of

I went to the cinema with Michael

You can add more information like:

My hair was combed into a beehive and my makeup was fresh from the Biba counter, the night I went to see 'Description' with Michael.

Part of your research should include reading other people's life stories. Browsing your local bookshop will show you what is being published at the moment and what type of life-story is popular. Look at those that are similar to the time or subject on which you are writing to see how well it has been written. See how facts are used to illuminate a period in someone's life.

Where to Go

If you are able to travel, revisiting the places in your life-story will be hugely beneficial. Places like schools, businesses, cinemas, theatres, parks and houses may all still be there and by revisiting them you can add better description to your story. If the area has changed greatly, look at old maps to locate yourself and the places that will feature in your writing.

Talking to local residents will revive your memories and provide you with new stories and other points of view. You might be able to look up old friends or family members. If you stay overnight, talk to the owners of the establishment and ask them for any suggestions on where you could conduct your research. There could be memorials or monuments that have been installed or a new exhibition or museum collection that will be worth visiting.

People are mines of information. We will discuss interviewing later in this chapter but if you are planning a visit, think of who might be interesting to talk to. Are there local historians or a local history club that could help out? Or prominent people in the neighborhood who will remember the times you are writing about?

If places no longer exist or you are unable to visit them, there are still lots of ways to check your facts. Libraries are great for checking information, by using books or their Internet facilities. Many also have microfiche with old newspapers and other documents available for viewing.

Museums and collections can refresh your memory about dress, fashion, art and many other subjects. Don't forget small local museums as well as town and national museums. Historical re-enactment days, open museums and military expositions can also give you a feel for the times you are writing about.

Photos are something that you will probably have to hand but they can also be of use as they can be printed in your article or book. Autobiographies often have one or two selections of photographs within them and magazines will always include a selection of images with a life-story it publishes. You can look out for photographic material at exhibitions and libraries. These may be copyrighted but if you can get permission to reproduce the photos, you will have more material for your story.

Records can be found in local archives, national archives, public records offices, church depositories and registrars of births, deaths and marriages. If you cannot visit these offices, you may well find the information you are looking for on the Internet.

Using the Internet

The Internet has become the easiest way to conduct research. It can be an extremely valuable tool if used with care, especially to refresh your memory about the news, film, music and world events. If you are a little computer shy, a friend or family member might like to do this kind of research for you.

However, the problem with the Internet is that it is not

regulated. Pages are put up with incorrect information or information that is out-of-date and no longer reliable. Any research you do on the Internet must be double-checked. You can do this by looking up different sources of information to clarify your research or checking what you find against books or documents covering the same subject area.

Nowadays there are some very high-quality genealogy websites that are packed full of records and databases for you to search. Some of these require a subscription fee or payment for viewing documents so be aware of any charges that you may incur whilst looking up information.

Maps can also be viewed online and the event of Google maps means you can walk around areas that are shown by the use of satellite images. This is a great way of revisiting places via the Internet if you cannot go there in person. You can also print off images and pictures of places that feature in your life-story and have them pinned up on the wall by your desk or in a place where they are easily seen to refresh your memory while you are writing.

Always remember to save information you find on the Internet with reference to the website and page you found it on. The Internet is a vast place and it is very easy to find something and lose it again just as quickly. Reference all Internet material so that you can find it again in a matter of seconds.

Checking Family History

In recent years, the interest in family history and genealogy has risen. This means there is much more information in public use than there ever was before. In the above section, we have mentioned using the Internet to check facts and link you to other people who may have information you can use. You can join forums or email relevant people to find out more.

Check out www.rootsweb.com, www.cyndislist.com and www.olivetreegenealogy.com/usa for American research and www.findmypast.com, www.genuki.org.uk and www.ancestry.co.uk for British searches. You will find other sites by browsing for genealogy or family history through your preferred search engine.

These sites contain information on births, deaths and marriages, emigration records, military records and census documents plus much more. In some cases, you can also view and contact other people who are researching the same information. This can lead you to family members and other people who have an interest in your research and could potentially have much to share with you.

The other way to check family history is to talk to family members and gather together any documents or historic materials they may have. If you cannot sit down and interview family members, you might be able to conduct phone interviews or email them a questionnaire with appropriate questions for them to answer.

Copies of certificates or documents could be emailed or faxed to you and that will save on posting out originals that may go astray. Ask your family to look in their attics, bottom drawers and stowed away boxes to see what family history might be uncovered.

Looking at World History

In chapter four, we looked at the bigger timeline perspective – what was going on in the world at the time your life-story was set. This is one of the areas where your research can run away with itself! You do need to know details about the world and what was happening in it but you don't need to know details about details.

What was the political and social background of the times? What was in the news? You can use the Internet to check dates and read old copies of newspapers online. Were there events happening that had people talking? Like war and conflict, mass unemployment or a recession? These events will impact on the characters that you have in your life-story writing. Think of the context in which they lived their lives. If there were strikes, major job-losses or a call for enlistment, they will have had an effect on people in your story whether they were directly involved or not.

Also consider famous people of the times. Events like the death of Princess Diana or the assassination of JFK had a profound effect on people. What were they doing when they heard of events like these? How did they react? What was the impact on the people around them?

Think about what is important in bringing your story to life. Is there a lot of social involvement in the story? Going out to theatres, picture houses or clubs? In that case, you will need to refresh your memory of what was playing at the time. What were the most influential plays and films? What bands did everyone want to go and see? What music was popular?

World history not only covers the political and cultural events of the time but all the little details that make up everyday life. To research world history, immerse yourself in the times. So for instance if you are writing a life-story that is set in the Seventies, watch TV and films that were popular then. Listen to music that evokes the era. Read books that were published at the time and look up books that have previously been written about life then.

Organizational Histories

If you are writing about a company or organization then you will need to get your hands on their documents and reports. If the company is still in existence, talk to the manager and explain to them what you would like to write. You will need a key contact that can supply you with documentation or give you access to their records. They can also put you in touch with people who have worked with the company who you can interview as part of your research.

Further information may be found in local museums and libraries. In the UK, company registration documents can be found at the Companies Registration Office or in the case of older records at the National Archives in Kew. In America, recent statements and periodic reports are kept by the EDGAR database that is compiled by the US Securities and Exchange Commission.

There are many smaller associations and societies that hold information on specific trades. They are a first stop for investigating a particular line of work and will have contacts so you can research them further. Search for them on the Internet using key terms that appertain to the organization you are interested in writing about.

Organizing your Research

When you conduct research, you will gather amazing amounts of paper! Folders, notebooks and box files easily become filled. Then you decide you really need that one bit of information and you have to search through all of it to find it.

Choose a way of organizing your research so you don't lose precious writing time searching. Start a new file or folder for each subject or area you are covering. So you might have one on buildings, dress, work or transport. If several characters appear in your story, you could have a file for each one that contains their biographies and other details you have collected.

Some files come with A-Z sections which can be useful for categorizing your work. Have a look in an office supplies or stationary store for the best solution for storing your research materials. Label everything and keep records of where you retrieved the information. By putting your research in order, you will be able to access particular information when you really need it.

If you have gathered family mementos, they can be a treasure trove of information to pass on to future generations or can be used as props if you are giving a talk on your life. Make sure you keep a list of all the mementos you have, who they belong to or who have donated them to you and any other details about them that you might need at a later date. Wrap delicate items in tissue paper and keep them all in a dust free box away from any direct sources of sunlight. Take especial care of old photographs and documents that are irreplaceable.

Interviewing

Interviewing can be used to check facts and add detail to your life-story writing. Say you want to include information about an old family member but you can't quite remember details, perhaps there is someone else in the family who does? Or if you are writing about an organization or company – who else was involved? Could you interview the manager, members or employees?

If your writing centers around a place, you could talk to the local post mistress, priest or schoolteacher. There are lots of people who could fill in gaps in your memory and give you more details and facts to write about.

Although talking about family history with your relatives may not seem like interviewing, if you do not record it in some way and structure your discussion to give you answers then when you come to write things down, key facts may be forgotten.

How to Prepare

With any interview, you need to contact your interviewee first and explain why you would like to talk to them. In order to do this, you need to be clear on your purpose and the aim of the interview. It could be a general aim, like talking to your grand-father about life during the Second World War or it could be more specific, like investigating his role as a pilot in the Air Force. The more specific you are, the more details you will get.

Before meeting your interviewee, list the questions you

would like to ask. Take a notebook, Dictaphone or digital recorder to record their answers but ask your interviewee permission to use them. You could also use a camcorder but this can make people nervous. Always check with your interviewee first.

If you cannot meet in the person's home or your own, choose a place where you can meet that is comfortable and free of distractions. Make sure there are suitable refreshments and access to toilets. Give yourself plenty of time to get to your destination and also to have a few minutes to clarify what you want from the interview before you head into it.

Conducting an Interview

Begin your interview by making the interviewee feel comfortable. Start by asking general questions to put them at ease. Make sure their personal details are correct and assure them that what they say is said in confidence. You will only use information in your writing that they agree can be published.

As they relax, you can delve more deeply into your subject matter. Give them time to reflect before answering your questions. If you rush an answer, it will not be as detailed as it could be.

If something is not clear or you want to double-check the information they are giving you, paraphrase their words and turn them into a question. For instance, they say that your Uncle Bert died in the Boer war. Ask them 'so was it the Boer war Uncle Bert died in?'

As the interview progresses, take down any notes of interesting information to come back to. Once people start talking and get caught up in their memories, it can be difficult to stop them and change the subject. Let them talk and then come back to the area that has sparked your interest when they have finished.

To end the interview, thank your interviewee and offer them a copy of the life-story or book that you are writing. If they ask to see what you have written about them before it goes to print, send them a copy. This can help iron out any irregularities before your work is printed.

Leave the interview by giving your full contact details if they do not have them already.

What to Ask

You will know from your own research and the structure of your book or story what details you need more information on. These could include facts about family members like appearance, habits, personality, work or hobbies. Your aim is to find out what they were really like so ask questions about their daily life as well as the main details.

You will want to check dates and places. Dates are not so easily remembered so ask for them but double-check them in the course of your research. When talking about places, try to get your interviewee to remember them using their senses so that you can build up good descriptions.

Ask open questions. These are questions that cannot be answered with yes or no. Open questions include the five W's of writing – who, why, what, where and when. Use them throughout the interview to gain more information.

There will be times when you want to find out more about a sensitive subject like a family secret or something traumatic that has happened. Treat these questions with care and do not push your interviewee too hard. They will tell you if they want to. If not, you will have to find out your information elsewhere. If your interviewee reacts by becoming distressed or upset, you will have to clarify with them if they will be okay with you writing about it. At the end of the interview, check with them that you can quote them in your life-story. You may not need to but it is always advisable to gain permission just in case.

Writing it Up

If you have just taken notes, write up the interview as soon as you can. Your notes will not be totally comprehensive so you should write out the interview while it is still fresh in your memory. Do not be tempted to add words in especially if you are going to use what is said in quotes.

Keep records of who you interviewed as you may need to go back to them or double-check facts with them if your life-story is printed. Keep the tapes or recordings safe and with the name, date and time of the interview.

Asking Permission

People may be happy to talk to you but they might not want to be identified or linked to your story. If they are happy to be quoted and you would like to use something they have said, you need to acknowledge them in your writing and double-check with them that it is ok to do so.

They may also allow you to use information as long as you do not disclose that it came from them. In this case, do not add anything into your writing that readers will recognize them by. At all times, adhere to an interviewee's wishes.

Chapter Eight

Editing and Presentation

You will need to revise and review your manuscript before it is ready to be sent to a publisher or editor. This means going over it, not just for mistakes, but to make sure you have included everything you had hoped to and that nothing has been left out, that the story reads well and the plot makes sense, that the characters are believable and so is the time and place – all these elements of your life-story need double-checking before your work enters the public arena.

This chapter looks at sending a book-length manuscript into a mainstream publisher. If you are going to produce your book yourself, read chapter nine. If you are only interested in writing magazine-length life stories then move on to chapter ten.

The Curse of the Red Pen

Do you remember having your work marked with a red pen at school? Red is the color of correction, whether you use a pen or the track changes function in Word. But it can be genuinely off-putting and disheartening to see your work so smattered in the color of a crime scene, even if you have done it yourself.

Lift the curse of the red pen and use another color! Try green or blue. They shout out 'we need changes here instead of 'you did it wrong, you're a bad writer'. You need to feel comfortable about revising and editing your own work and it will need revising. There is not a writer in the world that can write the first draft of a novel flawlessly. There will always be something that needs changing – a spelling mistake here, bad dialogue there, a series of zzzzzzzzz where your cat stepped on the keyboard when you weren't looking.

How to Review Your Own Work

The most important step in reviewing your own work is to put it away for a few days, two weeks if you can manage it, and leave it alone. Don't read bits. Don't think of things you could add in. Just leave it and forget about it.

How can I when I've spent months on it, I hear your cry. Because this is the only way you can look at it with fresh eyes, eyes that will see where the dialogue has slowed or the setting hasn't been described in enough detail. After a good length of time, dust off your manuscript and begin to read again.

(If you are reviewing your work on a computer, changing the page to full screen reading view can help change the way you look at your manuscript. This shows you what it will look like as two printed pages. However, you cannot edit text using this format.)

Once you begin your revision, you need to read through your life-story several times. First, read it for readability. Does the story make sense? Have you added everything in? Is there anything now you want to take out? Check that the timeline works and that the plot is effective. Make any changes that your life-story needs. If this involves rewriting whole chapters or large pieces of your story, don't worry, just do it. Your aim is to present your life-story to an editor or publisher, friends or family, as the best work you've ever written and if it needs more time, more tweaking, then so be it. Your story will be a better read for all the revision and editing you do to it.

Now read again and this time, check for emotion and pace. Does the story portray the feelings you hoped it would? Will the reader feel the emotions coming off the page? Does the writing feel paced? Are the highs and lows in the right places?

Is your beginning as exciting or interesting as you can possibly make it? Remember that readers will be hooked in by the first few sentences or not. Double-check that the start of your story leads the reader into wanting to know more, to carry on reading and to not put your book down. Then check your ending. Does it neatly tie the story up at the end? Does it conclude in a way that will satisfy your reader? Make any adjustments to emotions, pace, beginnings and endings that are needed.

By this time, you'll be on a third or fourth re-read but we've not quite finished yet! Review your descriptions and settings. Are all the places and faces well-described? Will a reader be able to picture them as you have seen them? Have you given enough information about your characters that they are brought to life for your readers? Does the dialogue between your characters sound real?

Once you are absolutely happy with the story in itself, read through for spelling, grammar and punctuation mistakes. Check that the vocabulary you have used is the best it can be. If you think you could have written it better, that a word just doesn't seem right, dig out a thesaurus and see if changing your vocabulary will improve your writing. Make sure you have avoided repetition so that your reader isn't bored by seeing the same words used over and over again.

And there you will have thoroughly reviewed your work. Once your changes have been made, put it away again and leave it to settle. Then give it the once over before sending it out.

Other People's Opinions

Do other people's opinions matter? Well, yes and no. If you have a friend who is in the publishing business, works as an editor or proof-reader then by all means ask them for their opinion. As professionals working in the industry, they will have a great deal of experience and expertise that they can share with you about your manuscript.

You can ask your family and friends to read your work and give you their opinion but remember they may not want to hurt your feelings so they might not offer much in the way of constructive criticism! By this stage, you have put a lot of work in and to receive unhelpful comments might undermine your wish to see your work in print.

The same goes for writer's circles and groups. These can be very supportive and useful to writers who wish to share their work but they can also have the opposite effect. If someone in your group doesn't like your work, it can have a negative effect on your confidence and self-esteem.

Accept other people's opinions only if they are constructive. Otherwise, leave it up to the professionals to decide whether your book is publishable or not.

Presentation of your Manuscript

Your life-story is written and it's ready to be submitted to an editor or publisher. You want it to look as good as possible on an editor's desk but don't go using brightly spotted paper, perfumed sheets or colored, bold text!

There is a format for presentation that manuscripts of every kind generally follow. Professionals will expect your work to be submitted in this appropriate manner. Publishers have style and format guidelines that will be given to you if your work is commissioned. However, if you are sending your manuscript in on spec, stick with a regular font like Times New Roman in 12pt, use double spacing and make clear where new paragraphs start. Either indent each new paragraph or leave a space between paragraphs. Use clean, white A4 size paper and bind your work using a paperclip and not staples. Check to see whether the publisher wants your work in hard copy, emailed or on disc as this could save you postage and print costs.

You will need to make up a title page that includes information that an editor can glance over. The title page acts as the top cover of your life-story. You must include your name, address, telephone number and other contact details on the left-hand top corner.

On the right-hand side, add your word count. Then centered in the middle of the page, add the title of your life-story on one line and your name underneath it. On the next sheet which will be the first of your life-story, put your address on the top right-hand side and center the story title and your name before starting on the main body of writing.

On the next and subsequent pages you need to write your surname, reference to your life-story and page number in the right-hand corner. For example: Watkins – My So Called Life (2). Use the header command if using a computer.

On the last page of the manuscript, add in the copyright symbol ©, your name and the year. This can be added as a footnote. For example: © Sarah-Beth Watkins, 2012.

Approaching Publishers

To find an editor or publisher, you can browse the Internet or look at The Writer's Market for American book publishers and the Writer's and Artist's Yearbook or The Writer's Handbook for British publishers. These compendiums are published yearly and contain information about book publishers, magazines and their requirements.

You can also check which publishers and magazines are producing and using life stories by browsing your bookshop. Look these up after you have found their names, either on the Internet or in the above compendiums, and you will find your submission information.

Checking out a possible publisher is a must. There is no point sending your work to a children's publisher or a publisher that only produces school textbooks. You need to find out who is publishing life stories and memoirs and how they can be approached.

As a general rule, publishers that take unsolicited submissions, will ask you to send in a cover letter, a chapter list, the first three chapters and a brief synopsis of your life-story. If they are interested in reading any more, they will ask you to submit the rest of the manuscript.

If the publisher does not accept unsolicited material, this means they will not read a whole manuscript that you send in yourself. They will only look at manuscripts that have been presented to them by an agent or they will only look at queries or ideas.

The Query Letter

A query letter is similar to a cover letter in that it needs to outline your proposed book and give some details of why you are qualified to write it. If you need to send out a query letter, make it as interesting or intriguing as possible. Try to attract the editor's attention to that they think – yes, I want to find out more.

Many publishers today allow queries through their websites by email or electronic form submission. You can still write a postal query letter but there may be some delay in replying to you or even any reply at all. Publishers are notoriously slow in replying to queries and submissions. If a publisher responds to your query and asks that you send in your life-story, you may not hear from them again for six months.

If your book is then rejected, you may get a personal response, a standard rejection slip or sometimes no contact at all. If you have not had any reply to your query in six months, you can take it that they are not interested in reading any further. If you have sent in a book manuscript and not heard from them in six months, email or write a gentle reminder to see if that gets a response. If you still don't hear back then send your work out to a different publisher.

The Cover Letter

We have said previously that publishers often want to see the first three chapters and a book synopsis before they decide whether to read an entire manuscript. These should be accompanied by a cover letter that sells your idea and introduces yourself.

A cover letter briefly introduces your work and can give any background information that is relevant. For example, you could write something like:

Please find enclosed the first three chapters of my life-story, My So Called Life, a love story set during the Second World War in London. This is a proposed novel of 55,000 words that examines what life was really like for young couples during the war years. From cardboard cake to GI nylons, this story details my relationships and the ultimate wedding-on-a-shoestring.

I have spent the past five years writing life stories. To date, I have been published in several local publications, Women at Home, Romance Weekly and Woman about Town.

I hope you will consider the enclosed for your imprint. Please do not hesitate to contact me should you need any further information.

If you have any writing experience, let the publisher know. Whether you have previously written a book, magazine articles or other forms of writing, tell them about your experience.

Also tell them if you have any expertise in the area you have written about. Ok, so it's your life-story but if as in the above example, it is set during a war and you are a history major, mention it in your cover letter. Any expertise or experience you have that is relevant to your book, include it. Sell yourself and your book at the same time.

The Synopsis

A synopsis is your story captured in a nutshell. Think of the blurb on the back of a book that gives you an idea of what the book is about; the bit you read before you make a decision to purchase it.

For your synopsis, write half a page that covers the main points of your life-story and includes details of place and time and your main characters. Try to summarize your life-story and capture all its main elements. Don't give the ending away or betray all the secrets your book contains. A synopsis is a little taste of what a book is about and should include intriguing statements that will make a publisher want to find out more.

Wrap it up with a statement such as – *the remarkable true story of a man who achieved his aims against the odds* – or something similar that captures your story in one sentence. This leaves a publisher thinking – how did they do that? And you will have hooked them into reading the full proposal.

The Chapter List

Hopefully, as you have been planning your life-story, you will have broken it down into chapters. Not all books have them, but they make it much easier to write a book-length manuscript by organizing the story into chunks. It is also better for the reader who has a place to put their bookmark and feels a sense of completion after reading each section of the story. Publishers will want to see a chapter list, which at a glance, shows them how the story pans out.

List your chapters numerically and give each chapter a title. Then summarize briefly what occurs in the chapter. Only use the main points. Keep it brief and succinct. Once you have the chapters listed, make sure that they show the story flowing onwards. Some writers find that when they do their chapter lists that some could be changed around to make the story flow more continuously and if that is the case, change them around in your full manuscript before you go any further.

The Submission

Once you have all the above together, you are ready to submit your work. Many publishers will accept manuscripts by email but you need to check with the publisher which method they prefer. They might have an electronic submissions system that you need to use or you may just need to email them files. Other publishers might want your work submitted on disc or as hard copy. If you are posting a hard-copy submission, enclose an SAE or international reply coupon if you want your manuscript returned.

Take a moment to congratulate yourself on getting this far. You have done all the hard work of writing your life-story, finding a possible publisher and making your manuscript presentable. It's time to put your feet up and relax!

Rejection

Unfortunately, all writers suffer from rejection. Publishers can turn down a book for many reasons. Their lists could be full, they have a similar book coming out soon, one of the same historical period was printed last year and so on. It doesn't necessarily mean that your work is no good, it just means it's not right for the publisher at that time.

If your life-story is rejected, send it out to another publisher. And keep sending it out until it hits its mark. If you get any feedback, work on it. A publisher might say they liked the story but found it was too slow – so look at the pace again. Or the characters weren't believable – so re-work your characters. Take on board any comments that the professionals make.

And if it keeps coming back? Then you might need to re-think your story or consider ways in which you can publish it yourself.

Chapter Nine

Getting Published

We have looked at how to approach mainstream publishers with your life-story but what if you want to do it yourself? You could produce your book on your own computer at home, use a print or self-publishing company or check out how to turn your writing into an e-book.

Doing it Yourself

You can produce your book at home using your own computer. You will probably be typing your life-story into word-processing software. Depending on the type of software and its functions, you can lay out your writing in book format.

Producing your own work means that you get to choose the font, the size of the text and you can insert your own images or photographs. You will need to be fairly computer literate to insert images and layout pages. Practice makes perfect but if it is really beyond you, perhaps there is someone in the family who can help?

One of the joys of producing your own work is producing your own cover. Again, using different software you can create a cover from the most basic image to a graphically designed masterpiece. You could scan in original photocopies or documents to use or work with an image that you have drawn or painted.

Don't forget the extras that make up a book like a contents page, a dedication, acknowledgements or an index. When you are producing your own work, you need to consider if any of these need to be included. One thing you will definitely need to include is a summary of your story on the back cover especially if your book is going to be for sale. Readers need an idea of what the book is about before they decide to purchase it. Write a short piece of approx. 200 words that captures your story and creates interest for a prospective buyer.

The quality of your book will depend on the printer and paper that you use. Higher-density paper with a gloss or silk finish will make the pages look more professional. Covers printed out on glossy card or photo paper will give the book a high quality look. Browse your local stationary store or office supplies shop for a selection of paper and card that you could use.

Paper comes in different weights and if you are including images, you may need a heavier weight so that the print doesn't show through to the next page. A heavier paper will also give your images a better picture quality. Try out different weights and finishes to see what works best for your book.

Your print run will depend on how many copies you need. Doing it yourself is best for a small print run when perhaps you are only going to give out copies to your family and friends. For larger print runs, you can save all your work on disc and check with a local print company how much they will charge to copy the amount you need.

Print companies nowadays offer much more than straight-forward copying. They can design your cover if you would prefer a professional touch or bind your book in different ways. When you use a printer, the more books you print, the lower the cost is per book. Ask for different rates, say 50, 100 and 200, as there may be very little difference between the larger print run amounts. Printing off a larger amount in the beginning may save you money in the long run.

Whether you print off your work yourself or use a printer's. Always check the first copy. You will have gone through several drafts as you were rewriting your life-story but double-check when your writing is in book format that everything is as it should be. This time look to see that the page numbers run sequentially, that the images are in the right place and that the cover looks fantastic. Only print your full amount once you are certain that everything is as perfect as it can be.

If you produce your own book, it may be difficult to sell. Main bookshops work with distributors and publishers, which does not leave much room for individuals to approach this type of retailer. There are other ways to sell your book, for instance, in your local shops, post office or supermarket – especially if the owners know you and you can also make sales through websites or advertisements placed in newspapers and magazines.

ISBN's

If you do want to sell your work, you will need an ISBN number – that's an International Standard Book Number. Before 2007, it was a 10-digit number but is now a 13-digit number that identifies your book to retailers and wholesalers. It contains a country code, publisher code, item number and check digit. Retailers use it to list your book and keep a track of its sales. If your book is being published by a mainstream publisher, they will be responsible for purchasing the number and having it displayed on your work.

ISBNs are purchased through agencies. The UK ISBN agency is Nielsen Book, www.isbn.nielsenbook.co.uk, and they are responsible for ISBNs in the UK and Eire. In The USA, the US ISBN Agency, www.isbn.org, is responsible for book numbers across the States. A quick Internet search will find your country's ISBN agency or look up the International ISBN Agency website at www.isbn-international.org to find your nearest agency.

There is a fee for purchasing ISBNs and you may have to buy a batch of them. In the UK, ISBN's are sold in batches of 10 whilst in the US, you can purchase them singly. Once you have an ISBN, you must display it on the back cover of your book and the reverse of the title page. More detailed guidelines are available from ISBN agencies.

Self-Publishing Companies

Using a self-publishing company can be an option for life-story writers. There are pros and cons to self-publishing. The biggest pro is you get your work published in book form without having to build up a portfolio or tout your work around publishers. But the other side to this is that you will be covering the costs for all aspects of the production of your book. However, this can suit life-story writers who only want to produce a small number of books for family and friends and want their work to be professionally produced.

Some self-publishing companies work on a print-on-demand basis. You only pay for the exact amount you need. Their services also include editing, proof-reading and design. This type of publisher is upfront about the costs you will incur and will be just as honest about how much they can be involved in marketing and distribution.

Vanity Presses

There are reputable self-publishing companies that produce high-quality books but there are also vanity presses that produce sub-quality work for a high fee. If you are considering paying a company to produce your book, rather than submitting it to a mainstream publisher or producing it yourself, you need to do your homework.

Vanity presses often pose as a mainstream publisher, asking to see your manuscript and agreeing to print it but there's the catch – they'll only print it for a fee. They often suggest that you work as a 'partnership' but really they are making their money from your payment and there will actually be very little that you do together in terms of making your book a saleable product.

Both vanity presses and self-publishing companies advertise in writer's magazines and it can be difficult to tell the difference between them. Get quotes from several companies and compare what they are actually offering you.

Ask to see examples of their previous publications so you can judge the quality of the print. Double-check how many copies of your book will be produced and at what price. Do they provide marketing and promotional services? Are they included in the price or are they extra? Are the books produced as paperbacks only or is there an option for hardback or e-book versions? Do they play a part in the distribution of the book or is that left entirely to the author?

Be very sure of what you are getting for your money before handing over your hard-earned cash. A self-publishing company will be upfront about what their services are and how much they cost. Vanity presses will be vague and try to flatter on one hand whilst holding out the other for payment.

Publishing Your Own E-Book

There are some websites that allow you to turn your book into a PDF file and post it as an e-book ready for sale. This is an extremely simple way of having your writing available as an e-book but most readers use Kindles or other electronic devices to read stories. If your book is Kindle compatible, it can be sold on Amazon websites and reach a much greater audience.

Kindle Direct Publishing gives authors online advice and guidelines for formatting their books. Check out their website at https://kdp.amazon.com.

To use KDP, you need to have an Amazon account. You can then access KDP and Author Central. Author Central lets you create an author profile that you can link to your books once they are uploaded to Amazon. KDP suggest that Microsoft users try Mobipocket Creator whilst Mac users can download Kindlegen. This free software will format your book ready to be uploaded to Amazon.

Once your book is formatted, it is uploaded to the bookshelf along with your book cover, pricing information, choice of royalties and your book details. You will be asked for information such as your genre, the edition number, whether it is part of a series or if you have an ISBN. ISBNs are not needed for e-books but KDP will give it an ASIN – an Amazon Standard Identification Number.

KDP isn't the only way in which to produce your work as an e-book but they are easy to use and there is help information for each step in the process. They also make your book available at a worldwide bookstore so your sales can begin straight away. If you are thinking of producing your work as an e-book, have a look at KDP for a step by step guide to producing your life-story e-book.

How to Decide What's Right for You

Deciding what is right for you can depend on several factors. The first is cost. How much do you have to spend on the production of your book? If the answer is little or nothing then you are looking at either sending your work to a mainstream publisher in the hope that you will receive a book contract or you could do it yourself by purchasing ink and paper to run off copies from your home computer. If you are willing to self-finance your project then using a print or self-publishing company might be the right decision for you. Think about whether you wish to contribute to the costs of producing your book and how much you can afford to invest in it.

The second is your level of computer literacy. In order to print off your own book, you will need to feel comfortable and have the skills to use a word-processing programme and elements of design. Assess whether you feel competent to do this or if there is someone who can help you produce your own work. Making your life-story writing available as an e-book requires another set of skills but they can easily be learnt from taking part in the process. Think about whether you feel confident enough to use the computer and Internet to give it a try.

The next factor is the amount of books you want to produce. For a small print run, doing it yourself can be the answer. Say, for instance, you just want ten books produced to give to your family then producing them yourself will be less costly than using a printer's. However, print-on-demand companies also accept small print jobs but for a fee. If you want your book widely available and distributed to main retailers then you need to look for a publisher or self-publishing company that can offer you the service you need.

Quality is also an aspect in determining how to produce your book. Doing it yourself can produce good-quality books but publishing companies have far better design and editing capabilities at their finger-tips. There is quite a difference between a book published by a mainstream company and one that has been run off at home. Decide how much quality matters to you and how you would ideally like your book to be presented.

Whether you want your book to be available as an e-book or paperback is also a consideration. Many authors today go straight for the e-book option, bypassing publishing companies, and doing it for themselves. As we've discussed, this takes a level of skill and the commitment to turning your writing into an e-book. It's definitely worth looking into if you are just printing off copies for family but would like to see if there is any interest from the general public. Some authors have gone on to have their books published by mainstream book publishers after the success of their e-books.

And finally whether your book is for sale or just for family is another factor for your consideration. Doing it yourself or using a printer's to make copies for your family will give you a book for personal use. If your book is going to be for sale, you will need an ISBN and some route for marketing and distribution. You will also need to think about how you will promote your book and get it into the public arena.

Cost, amount, quality, production type, the market you are aiming for and how widely you wish your life-story to be available are key factors in helping you to decide what is right for you.

Copyright

Copyright is the law surrounding the ownership of intellectual property. It means that any article, book or story that you write cannot be used without your permission. Copyright determines the rights of the author as the owner of his or her material. It stays with a writer for his or her lifetime and 70 years after their death. Copyright covers the work you have produced but not titles or ideas.

When you put the internationally recognized copyright symbol along with your name and date on a piece of your writing, you are asserting your rights as an author and you therefore have the right to sell, reproduce or edit your work in any way you wish. Other people, however, can't, and if found doing so will be in breach of copyright law unless you have sold your copyright to them.

In the same respect if you copy another author's work, known as plagiarism, without permission you will have breached the copyright laws. You can be sued for this so it is essential you always write in your own words. If you need to include song lyrics, photographs or written passages that are not your own, seek permission from the owner and check whether you need to pay any copyright fees.

Remember to include copyright information to protect your own work. The copyright symbol © is followed by your name and the date the work was produced or copyright invoked, as follows – © Sarah-Beth Watkins, 2012. When selling your life-story you should rarely ever be asked to sell your copyright but you may be asked to sell other rights. Magazines often ask for country-based serial rights and web-page editors will ask for electronic rights.

Every piece of work you send out should have copyright information on it. Magazines and newspapers are reputable companies and problems over copyright rarely happen. However, your work should be protected in case of query. Always keep an original copy.

Libel

You could be liable for defamation of a person's good character if, for instance, you have turned them into a villain or portrayed them as a psycho killer. It doesn't even have to be as dramatic as that. Any inference you have made, however small, that causes personal offence, could land you in trouble. Using libel or defamatory insults could involve you in a court case.

This can be difficult for a life-story writer, especially if you are dealing with traumatic or emotional aspects of your life. Writing about the people that have influenced you or colored your life in some way will not always be a bed of roses. Not everyone will have contributed to your life in a positive way and in some cases, will have had very extreme negative effects.

Libel laws are different across the globe so we would advise anyone who is self-producing a book that will be in the public domain to have it checked by a solicitor. In the UK, libel isn't the only issue; there are also laws against blasphemy, sedition and obscenity. Obscenity speaks for itself but blasphemy and sedition are laws that you rarely hear of.

Blasphemy involves the criticism of the Bible and the Christian religion. This may seem antiquated given that we live in a multi-denominational world but it allowed Salman Rushdie's publishers to produce the Satanic Verses, a book that condemned the Muslim religion. If it had been about the Christian religion, it would have been perceived by UK law as blasphemous.

Sedition is a law that protects the government and royal family. If a book is deemed seditious and likely to disturb the peace, the writer can be prosecuted. It is rare for these laws to be enacted these days but you should be aware of them as a writer to ensure there are no legal issues surrounding your work.

Chapter Ten

Writing Life Stories for Magazines

Magazines come in all shapes, sizes and subject areas. Newspapers have regular supplements on a variety of topics. Columns are written on every subject from driving to country living. The freelance market is so wide and varied, there is always room for life-story writing.

Take a look at the shelves in a newsagent's the next time you are out shopping. Just pause to look at the range of magazines that are on offer. Then look closer at the ones that appeal to you, the ones you read or are on subjects you could write about. The knowledge and experience you have gained from life is a valuable asset when writing for the magazine market.

Writing Life Stories for Magazines

There are two types of life stories that are regularly published in magazines. The first are personal, first-person viewpoint pieces written in a story format and the second are factual articles that are based on your knowledge and experience.

You may want to concentrate on a book-length manuscript but writing stories and articles for magazines can help you to practice your life writing skills and may earn you a substantial income.

They are of a much shorter length, from a few hundred words to a few thousand, so they can be completed in a shorter period of time. This helps you to boost your confidence as a writer by having work finished and editor ready in the space of weeks rather than months or years.

Having your life stories published in magazines also gives you an attractive portfolio to refer to when approaching book publishers. A writer that has had several life stories already in print shows proof of their skill and ability; something every book publisher likes to see.

Researching the Magazine Market

From looking in a newsagents, you will see that there are hundreds of magazines and hundreds of markets for you to write for. You will need to research this market for the best magazine to send your work to. It is a waste of your time and effort to send a story or article to the wrong magazine.

You need to make sure that your article is suitable for the magazine or newspaper that you send it to. We have mentioned previously using guides like The Writer's and Artist's Yearbook or Writer's Market. They contain an A-Z of British and US magazines and newspapers that includes contact names and addresses, whether they take freelance contributions, information about word lengths, types of article and the magazine's requirements.

However, using these guides are no substitute for your own research. Magazines can go out of print, new ones hit the shelves, editors change and so do freelance possibilities. You need to keep an eye on the magazine market for opportunities by browsing newsagents and booksellers regularly.

Before thinking of a magazine as a possible place to sell your work, check first to see if they take freelance contributions. One way is to find the company information; address, telephone numbers, copyright, etc (usually printed near the editorial). Along with this information, it may state something like 'submissions are made at the writer's discretion and the magazine is not liable for the return or use of such manuscripts'. Or it might state that they do not accept unsolicited manuscripts. This means they won't look at anything you send them without being approached with the idea first.

The Story Format

The story format is used to tell a reader some part of your life-story; to tell of a time in your life or an event that you have experienced. They concentrate on one occasion rather than being spread out across a life-story timeline. They are written in the first person, 'I', and are usually in the region of 800 – 2,000 words as full-page features although smaller pieces are often used. Looking at various magazines on different subject areas will show you the word length that suits a particular magazine and the subject areas that people's life stories cover.

Life stories are used to tell tales of childbirth, child rearing, romance, relationships, crime, nostalgia, medical stories and much more. A story about childbirth might appear in a parenting magazine or a romantic liaison in a woman's publication. First-person viewpoint pieces turn up within the pages of many magazines alongside their factual articles.

Some magazines concentrate only on life stories and use a chatty and informal style to relate to their readers. These magazines are packed with real-life stories, tips, advice and relate directly to the reader, inviting them to send in their own stories. They will have particular sections like health, crime, and relationships that you can submit your life stories to.

They may also ask for photographs to complement your story so be prepared to send in accompanying images if they are asked for.

The Article Format

Factual articles can be written based on the knowledge and experience of a subject that you have gained over the course of your life. The best way to decide on whether factual article writing is for you is to consider your topic. What can you write about with insight and authority?

Choosing Your Article Topic

Here's an exercise that might help you to clarify what area of your life to concentrate on. Set out a page with three columns, *topic, research* and *magazine*. We shall come back to the magazine column but for now let's look at the first column marked topic. Under that column, list everything you feel comfortable writing about, that you have life experience of and that you know you could write about confidently.

In the second column, *research,* you can consider what elements of that subject you would have to do some more research on. For instance, you might have raised a family and have a wealth of knowledge about caring for small children. You want to write a piece on child-raising in the 1950s compared to the present day but you need to bring yourself up to speed with the latest developments. In that case, you will need to research childcare today.

Let's look at another example – gardening, for instance. You've been a keen gardener for many years. You have your own vegetable plot and know when it's time to sow, plant out, transplant and harvest. You've dealt with problems of pests and blight. There's a wealth of knowledge here that you could use to write an article.

You could write articles for gardening, country life or farming magazines. Your local newspaper might be interested in a gardening column. Your Parish or church journal might consider a piece on what grows best in your locality.

Now for the third column, *magazine.* See what markets might be available to your subject. Add into this column, magazines you know of or have seen in your trips to the newsagents. These are your possible markets. Do your market research and you will know the best magazine to approach with a factually based article.

Writing An Article

Articles can be split into three sections; beginning, middle and end. As well as the main body of your text you will also need a title and possibly quotes and side-bars. We shall look at how to use these to create an in-depth piece of work.

Titles

Editors can be very fussy about titles. The attraction of titles become apparent when you realize that that is what draws you to a magazine and is usually what you scan over when deciding whether to buy it or not.

Make your title outstanding. Take time over what you choose. It's going to be the first thing that an editor reads before he or she looks at your article. You need to attract them to your work too. If they have a stack of 15 articles that need reading, whose will be first out of the pile with a snappy title?

Use puns on words, catchy sayings, rhyming phrases – something that stands out and draws you into reading more. Sometimes 2 or 3 words can be the catchiest. But don't spend more time on your title than you do on your article!

Unfortunately even the best-thought-out titles can end up on the editor's cutting-room floor. They can and will change the title of an article if they feel it's not quite right for the tone of their magazine.

Beginnings

The beginning of an article is probably the most important part. It is the hook that attracts the reader, drawing them in and giving them a taste of what's to come. In the first two or three sentences you have to make the intentions of the article clear.

You can start by writing a few catchy sentences or use one of three tricks of the trade. Number one, pose a question that will intrigue readers and make them want to know the answer. The answer is of course contained in the rest of your article but they will be sufficiently interested by the right start to read the whole piece.

Number two, hit your readers with a fact. Use something shocking or startling, something that will make people double-take. Examples of typical starts are: *In a recent poll, 25% of young adults males said...* or *One in 10 American women have.....* or *By the time you're 30 you will have......*Use a fact to open up your article and then lead into your main topic.

Number three, open up an article with a topical quote. The more influential or high profile the person or organization you use a quote from the better. You don't have to only quote the famous. How many times have you read 'a spokesperson for so and so said....'? Just choose your spokesperson well. Contact managers, directors, professors, doctors – professionals who are experts in their field when looking for a quote.

Just remember that whomever you quote you must do so word for word. You don't want to risk legal proceedings over libel and misquoting. Never be tempted to put words in to quotes to make them sound better or more interesting. Only use a quote that you know is correct.

Make sure that whatever way you start your article, you make it sound interesting and that interest will make your readers read further.

Middle

You've written an amazing beginning, now you need to continue your article. No-one can write it for you so only practice will get it right. Keep paragraphs small and sentences short. Remember to write clearly and concisely. Write tight!

Use the 5 W's – who, why, what, where, when – to unravel your article. Pace your article well. If you have 1,200 words to write perhaps you might use the first 50 in really attracting your reader, the next 200 on the main points, use the body of text to explain the background and unravel the subject and then use the last 150 words to sum up.

Articles are not essays. Where an essay has a clear intro-duction, main points and conclusion, articles don't. Articles are top heavy. You want to use your best facts, the most amazing revelations, the crucial information all closer to the beginning than the end. Some people only ever read the first few paragraphs of an article to glean the general information it contains. How many times have you read a newspaper article because it looked interesting but you never quite made it to the end?

End

That doesn't mean to say you must neglect your ending. Editors are not going to publish articles that trail off indefinitely. Tie up your article by clarifying its overall theme.

Use the last two or three sentences for an upbeat comment for a happy piece, a significant statement for serious piece.

Style and Tone

Articles vary not only in subject but in style, tone and length. Style is something you will develop for yourself. It is unique to you and you might not even realize your own style until several articles later. Editors will either like it or not but if you've done your research, it will at least be in keeping with their type of magazine. Each magazine has its own tone and this is based on the market that they are aiming for, their type of readers.

Article length is also very important and can even be the decider in whether your piece is read let alone used. Editors work with spacing. They have to make their magazine presentable and legible. An average article is approx. 1,000 – 1,500 words long and will cover two pages with photographs. A one page article with little illustration would be 800 – 900 words. Fillers are mini articles of 250 – 300 words that are used to fill gaps. Columns are also around 250 – 300 words.

Each magazine has its own slots and your market research will show you what length of article goes where. Unfortunately the only way to ascertain word length is by counting – manually! As a rough guide though there are usually 10 words per line so you can estimate on that basis.

It may seem a chore but article length is important. If you send a 1,500-word article to an editor that never uses more than 1,200 in any one piece, you risk having your manuscript returned unread. Editors are too busy to cut and polish every time. If they have an urgent gap in the magazine and two articles arrive that morning one of the correct word length and one that would need trimming down, what one are they likely to use?

Doing your market research and putting your findings to good use improves the chances of your article being accepted. Small things like word length may seem trivial but they can be crucial to an editor's decision.

Letters to the Editor, Fillers, and Columns

One of the easiest ways to get your name in print is by writing a 'letter to the editor'. Magazines and newspapers all have letters or opinion pages where you can write in and express your feelings on the magazine or the subject matter they've covered.

Letters are used more frequently than articles. Editors can keep articles on file for months but letters are used quickly because they are topical and only usually relevant to the next issue.

Letters are a good filler for you to use when working on an article for some light relief or when you are in between articles or need a break from working on your book manuscript.

One type of 'letter to the editor' is the personal viewpoint. If you read an article that rings true for you, that you have some experience of, then let them know. In the same respect, if you read an article that you disagree with , that contains assumptions that annoy you or facts that you are shocked by, then tell the magazine.

Typical starts to these letters might be: *With reference to your article in June's issue of Blah Blah Monthly, I feel I have to share my experience with you...* or *Congratulations! Your article on ....was terrific. I just wanted to let you know......*

You can also use letters to tell your personal stories. If something humorous has happened to you that will bring a smile to readers faces (and you're not too embarrassed about sharing it) then write it down. Letters telling of sad, tragic or courageous are also used, especially if in response to a previously published article. You need to do the ground work first, read the magazines or newspaper, find something you can comment on enthusiastically and then send off your missive.

Bear in mind the tone and style of letter you write should be in keeping with the magazine you are writing to. Letters should be short and to the point. Editors, however, will trim and edit letters to fit into the page.

Fillers

Fillers are mini articles, very short pieces that are used to fill gaps. They are usually only 250 – 300 words but can be shorter or longer depending on the space they need to fill. Market research is important when trying to place fillers. Some magazines use them often, others rarely.

Fillers are written like articles but because of their length writing has to be concise and to the point. There is no room for flowery description or long-winded explanations. Topics for fillers vary and you will have to look for writing opportunities in the magazines that appeal to you.

Columns

Columns are short, mini articles that give a personal opinion or viewpoint. They are easy to write as they are based on your life experiences but can be harder to have accepted for publication.

Columnists have usually been working for a magazine for some time or have a long background in freelance writing that leads them to being offered the opportunity to write in this style.

However, if you have a great idea for a column then there's nothing to stop you from approaching magazines or newspapers that lack a column on a particular subject. Send the editor 3 or 4 examples of your work and a cover letter that details any experience you have that is relevant. For instance, you might have worked as nurse for several years and could write a medical column or have worked in an animal health center so could write on aspects of pet care.

Tips and Suggestions

Tips and suggestions are another way of using your life knowledge and experience to reach a reading public. Many magazines have tips pages especially the specialised knowledge magazines like gardening, DIY, pet care, etc.

Again looking at magazines to find opportunities is your best bet. Whenever you see '£20 offered for tips' or '£50 used for our star letter', cut it out and keep it in a clippings file. When you've got a spare moment or something springs to mind, look at your clippings file for somewhere to send your work.

The great thing about letters, tips and suggestions is that they only cost the price of a stamp to submit or you may be able to submit them online. You can easily find the time to write these and even magazines that don't take freelance contributions will take tips and suggestions.

Submission and Presentation

Magazines that use a lot of life stories may have a submission form online or in the magazine that you can use to send in your idea. If it's something that hasn't been used before or is an interesting take on an old subject, an in-house writer will contact you and work with you on the story. Alternatively, you can send in your complete story and wait for feedback.

Articles and life stories that are submitted to magazines and newspapers in hard copy follow the same guidelines we discussed in chapter eight but you only need a cover letter, a title page and the full article.

A title page is a sheet that sits in front of your article and contains your details, the title of the article, the word count and what serial rights are being offered. Add your name, address, email and any other contact details on the top left-hand side of the page. Opposite this, on the right-hand side of the page, add your word count and the serial rights offered.

Serial rights are offered in the country the magazine you are writing for is based, so if you are sending your work to a UK magazine, you would offer First British Serial Rights. First denotes that the article has not been published elsewhere. If it has been sold to another magazine before, you would offer second rights.

In the middle and center of the title page, add in the title of the article and your name. Attach it to your article and include a cover letter before posting out to a magazine or newspaper editor.

Chapter Eleven

Writing Life Stories for Others

Writing life stories and family histories for other people is a great way to practice your writing and research skills. Writing stories for others is also a less solitary occupation than being a writer usually is. Meeting with other people to research a book or having many face to face conversations with a particular family member makes this type of writing much more sociable and you will be helping someone, who otherwise would not be able, to tell their life-story.

Helping Others Tell their Tales

Who could you help? There are many people who have a tale to tell who would love some assistance in getting their stories written down, whether to pass onto their own families or to have published. Friends and family are all likely candidates but also think further afield. Do you know someone in your community who has had an interesting life? Or could you help members of a retirement group or elderly day-care center to work on their life stories? In the next chapter, we will give you tips and advice for running your own workshops and designing writing courses that could be delivered to such groups. But are their individuals you could offer your skills to? Helping others to write their life stories is challenging but can be immensely rewarding.

Working on a life-story with another person will take organization and planning. To find out the details of their life, you will need to have many conversations and to research the historical times in their lives for consistency and clarity. Older people's memories may be confused so double-checking facts and details will be an essential part of writing their life stories.

Recording your conversations will be essential. There is no way you will be able to write it all down verbatim. Of course you can take notes but in doing so you may miss key elements of their story while you are concentrating on your notepad. Invest in a Dictaphone or digital recorder and make sure that each file or tape is dated correctly as you progress through the tales of their life.

When you come to writing up their story, your recordings will be your main source of information but you will still need to add in background facts, authentic settings and good characterizations. That's where your research will come in and help to flesh out their life-story into a believable tale.

When it is all written up, it is advisable to give a copy to the person you are helping. You can print it off in large print for elderly readers or make a recording of yourself reading out the story. As with any life-story writing, there will be the need to re-draft and review the material and it is surprising how much more information will be offered once a person reads or hears their story for the first time.

Be prepared to help with the publication side of things. You might be asked to help find a publisher or to print off copies for their friends and families. They might even want you to arrange their book launch! These extras are all part of helping other people to tell their tales from beginning to end.

Whether you ask for a fee is between yourself and the person you are writing about. If you are not a well-published author then to ask for payment at this stage in your career is probably not appropriate. Helping others should not always come at a price.

Ghost-writing

If you want to make money from writing life stories then ghost-writing could be for you. Ghost-writing is a professional service that a writer offers other people for a fee. Ghost-writers have written many of the autobiographies of famous stars and celebrities who are either too busy or are too unskilled to write for themselves. You never know who the ghost-writer is as they are never credited with what they have written. Their names are not linked with a book and only the celebrity's name appears on the cover.

Often a once-off fee is negotiated between an agent and the ghost-writer. They are given a contract for the work only and not for any ongoing connection to its sales. The writer then has no claims over the book or article and does not have any legal grounds concerning copyright. So why write if you are not going to be acknowledged for it? The fees that agents pay can be quite substantial. If you are interested in this line of work, you can contact agents outlining your experience and skills and ask for consideration for future projects. Agents who regularly work with celebrities often have a database of ghost-writers to use when such a project comes up.

It is a way of earning an income that leaves you free to pursue your own writing projects. Some ghost-writers are authors in their own right and of completely different genres. Writing for other people is just another way of making a living without their name being associated with writing that differs from their own.

Writing Family History

Who in your family has an interesting life-story to tell? Think of all the stories that have passed down in your family, of special people, events and occasions. Is there someone whose story would make for an amazing and interesting read?

It could be a relative who is still alive and you can therefore work with them to produce their own life-story or it could be stories of your long dead ancestors that will need researching. If you want to write your family history, you will need to start by compiling your family tree. Investigate each generation using genealogy resources to build a true and accurate picture.

In chapter seven, we looked at where to go to look for facts and how to check out your family history. Joining top quality genealogy forums and websites will give you a link to online records and databases that will be invaluable in your research. If you can visit archives and record offices, do, but you will also find a wealth of information on the Internet including original scans of military records, census information and immigration lists.

This kind of research will generate lots of paperwork so keep your files organized. You could have a file for each family member or family unit that you add to as information turns up. Investigating your family tree will always turn up surprises. Often the stories we are told as we are growing up have changed over time, been added to, or parts missed out. Relatives you never knew you had will turn up and occupations, locations and family connections will be revealed. It is essential to keep track of what you find.

Writing a family history into a book format takes time and commitment. Research can take as much time if not more than the actual writing does. Try not to get swamped in research and schedule time which is purely for writing.

The most important element of writing a family history is its structure. You will need to decide early on in which way the information you find will be presented. Will you write a chapter on each of the prominent members of your family? Or use each chapter to concentrate on one branch of the family? Perhaps you might like to just write your family history in a linear fashion starting with the youngest member or the oldest member you have traced. Decide on your structure so that as you build on your research you know how you are going to use it and in which chapter it will appear.

Don't forget you might also want to include images or photographs. Documents can be scanned into your computer and placed amongst the text or included as a color insert. Be careful not to mark originals especially if they are borrowed from other family members.

Consider how you will publish your family history. It is unlikely you will find a mainstream publisher to print your book unless it includes a noteworthy historical character or is based around a particular world event or time in history. The likelihood is that you will be self-producing your family history whether you print it yourself or use a reputable company.

Stories for your Grandchildren

One of the most delightful ways to write up your life stories is in the form of a book for grandchildren and other young people. Writing for children is an art in itself and if you are considering writing up a life-story so that it appeals to younger generations, your key decision will be to decide what age range you are aiming for.

Will it be a picture-book for others to read to children? Or an early reader, using basic language, for them to read to themselves? Perhaps you could write a teenage fiction that is based on elements of your life-story? Have a look in your local library or bookstore at the kind of books that children are reading at present and decide which would best suit your story.

A typical picture-book is produced using pages in multiples of eight and averages at thirty-two pages. Pictures are the main ingredient as the text in a picture-book is quite short at approximately 300 - 500 words. Mainstream publishers usually accept a picture-book for publication and assign an artist to illustrate it but if you are producing the book yourself, you can use your own drawings or paintings or ask another family member to illustrate it for you.

Writing a story in 500 words can be more difficult than you think. A picture-book has to contain all the elements of a story in so few words and appeal to young children. The best way to see how picture-book text works is to read several stories. Some favor repetition, others use poetry and some have straight-forward stories. You will need to consider the best format for the story you wish to tell.

Books for beginner readers should use language and vocabulary that they are familiar with. Early readers are short, 300 – 500 words and often use repetition so that readers become used to certain words. That doesn't mean that the stories are boring and repetitive but that they are written for a particular reading level that you should be aware of when writing up your life-story for a younger generation. Children usually begin to read around the age of five which coincides with the start of formal education in schools. Sentence structure is simple and kept short and any ambiguous words should be avoided. Writing for beginner readers is about producing a story that is well-written but suitable for a child's early literacy levels.

Books for older readers vary in length and subject matter. Look at children's book publishers to see if your story would fit into one of their series or imprints. Most publishers have different slots for different age ranges. Examine several books in a series to gauge whether your life-story could be written up in a way that suits. If you are hoping to write for children, read what others have written and what is popular in the age range you are aiming for.

If you have children in the family, find out what they like and what they want to read about. Let them tell you what stories they enjoy. When you have something written up, try it out on them. Watch their reactions. Are they excited, interested to know more? Or bored and their attention wandering? Children will easily let you know whether your story is working for them or not. You can use their feedback to adjust your story before printing or publishing your work.

Books for teenagers nowadays are not much different from those for adults. The word length can be the same and the subject matter just as intense or in-depth. A lot of the stories involve coming-of-age or developing from a child to a young adult but this is not always the case. You may have had interesting formative years that you could use as the basis for a teenage story or perhaps there are elements of your life-story that would make a good tale for today's teenagers. Looking again at the market and the stories that teenagers are reading is essential research if you are considering writing for this age range.

Writing your life-story in a format for children to read can be a great way to pass on your life knowledge and experience to younger readers.

Writing Biographies

Biographies are the stories of an individual as told by another person. They concentrate on a person's life against their historical background. Many biographies are heavy on history but they still contain elements of fiction. Facts are used throughout to place and date the person's life but sometimes a writer needs to fill in the gaps and presume what might have happened at such and such a time.

They can be about anyone – to a point. Choosing a subject for a biography needs careful consideration. For one, you are going to have to research this person and the time of their lives in great detail, finding out everything there is to know about them. This takes time and commitment as we have mentioned before but you also need to find this person so fascinating that you never become bored of their story. Make sure when choosing your biographical subject that you can stay with them for the duration of their tale.

The other consideration is whether anyone else will find your subject interesting. There are some people in history who have had numerous biographies written about them; Oliver Cromwell, Elizabeth I, Marie Antoinette, General Custer, the list goes on. You can choose to write a biography about someone who has been written about before as long as you bring something new to the mix. Perhaps you've discovered new documents or have a particular view about a shadowy part of their lives that you could illuminate in a fresh way. Whatever it is, it has to be different from the many books that have gone before.

You might be thinking the safe bet would be to write about someone who has never had a biography written about them. Surely a publisher would jump at that chance? Unfortunately, that is not necessarily the case. If a publisher cannot gauge the interest of readers by the popularity of similar books, they may not want to take the chance with a complete unknown. Of course, you can self-publish if you wish but to attract a mainstream publisher, a biography must be based on the life-story of someone that they are certain the public will want to read about.

Writing biographies uses many of the techniques we have discussed already. The timeline will be an important starting point so that you can place your individual in the correct historical setting and see where you need to undertake research. Your research will combine reading what has been previously published, any original manuscripts you can find, looking at books that describe the times and numerous other avenues that will occur as you are writing. If you can visit the places that you are writing about, all the better, as it will give you a feel for your story. Don't forget museums, re-enactments and other historical open days to give you a true glimpse of what people wore, ate, slept on, lived in, etc.

Double-check your facts meticulously. When you are writing a family life-story, there are not many people who can contradict what you have written, unless it is other members of your family. Biographies are different in that academics will read them, people who have made it their life's work to investigate a certain period in time, and they will shout loudly if your facts are wrong. If you can get an expert to help you with your research, give you tips or pointers, or read through your work for authenticity, then their help will greatly improve your writing. It might just mean sending an email every now and again to check on something you are not sure of but having an expert or two to call on will be a great asset.

You will be expected to have all the material you have used correctly referenced. Have a look at the back of some biographies to give you an idea of how references work. There are references listed that have been marked in the text. As you are writing you will reference a quote or some material that you have used in brackets, these will then be compiled at the back of the book in full so that if people want to check the facts you have included, they can locate the original material. Then there is usually a reference book list or further reading list, which supplies readers with all the books you have used for your research and that they can continue to read if they want to investigate the subject further. Finally, there will be an index that can be quite comprehensive and may be compiled by yourself or a professional indexer.

Chapter Twelve

Passing on your Skills

In this final chapter, we shall assume that you have been writing and during the process you have gained skills that could be passed on to others. Whether you have been writing short life-stories, human-interest articles or concentrating on a full-length book, you have begun your career as a life-story writer. You could now share your experience and knowledge with others who would like to learn more about writing life stories and promote your own work at the same time.

Recognizing the Skills you've Gained

What have you learnt? What has the process of writing given you, in the way of new skills and knowledge? Take time to consider all the elements of writing you have mastered. It could be that you now know how to use a timeline, can make up a plot structure, bring characters to life and know how to write good descriptions and settings.

Or what about those research skills you have gained? You can list good resources and the not so good. You know where to go to find documents and records whether online or in your locality.

And don't forget to recognize the skills you have gained from the publishing process. If you have done it all yourself, think of all the skills you now have. Whatever experience you have gained from approaching the publishing industry can be passed on as valuable information to new writers.

Giving Talks

One of the best ways to pass on your knowledge is by giving a talk. Some writers are approached to talk to attendees at a conference or to give a presentation as part of a week-long writing event. In this case, you might be asked to speak on a certain topic or part of the writing process. The subject matter is given to you and a time allocated for your talk.

You can also offer your services to organizers of functions and events for writers or make it known in your local community that you are available to give talks to groups, clubs and centers.

Public speaking can make many people nervous but if you plan your talk well in advance and are comfortable with your topic it will make things easier. If you are giving a talk, always know your time allocation – is it 10 mins, 20 mins or longer? Once you have your talk length, you can start to work out the best way to present your material. You can even use quotes or passages from your work during talks.

Start by writing it all out. Just get your thoughts down on paper and then practice talking aloud whilst timing your speech. Cut and revise as you mould your writing to its time slot.

The more you practice reading your speech out aloud, the easier it will flow. You can take your written speech with you or just put pointers down on a small card so that you are reminded of the structure of your talk as you are giving it.

Be prepared for a questions and answers session after the talk. Although you will never be entirely sure what you are going to be asked, have the confidence in your own abilities to be able to answer questions as informatively as possible. You know more about your subject than your audience so share your knowledge with them.

Promoting your Work

Ok so you might not want to hard sell your book or short stories but every opportunity you have to talk to the general public, give a workshop or deliver a course, puts you in the public eye. There you are a real-life writer who has gone the distance and seen their work in print. People will want to read what you have accomplished.

You can have copies of your book available at talks and workshops. There's no need to push their sales. Have them available, perhaps at a reduced price, on a table where attendees will see them.

Being published is proof of your writing ability. You can use copies of your work as part of a CV if you are showing prospective clients or use them to give students an idea of what has worked during analysis sessions. Be aware of blowing your own trumpet though! Handing out your work with a 'look how great I am' attitude will not go down well with your learners.

What about a Workshop?

One step up from a talk is the workshop. This is a more inter-active session usually with a smaller group. It could be a one off you have arranged yourself or may be part of a writer's event or day of workshops where people chose which topic they would like to work on the most.

The length of a workshop can vary but is usually between 2 – 3 hours. Timing again is essential in structuring a workshop session. It is a good idea to time each part of the workshop. So for instance, meeting and greeting may take 5 mins, getting people to introduce themselves and say a bit about their own writing experience may take a further 10 mins, your introduction may take 10 mins more and so on. Break the workshop down into time slots so that you are confident that everything will be covered in one session.

In order to decide what to cover, you need to consider the theme of the workshop. In such a short space of time, what do you hope to pass on to your participants? The overall aim will help you to plan the workshop so that each person comes away from it having learnt something new or having tried something different.

Workshops are interactive. You will need tasks and exercises for participants to accomplish and a space for them to discuss their findings afterwards. These can be anything from writing tasks to role plays to group games.

Say your workshop is just based on an introduction to life writing. You might want to share with participants how to use a timeline and begin researching their history. So you do a written exercise on timeline plotting then you ask participants to get creative by drawing a section of their timeline. Next you ask for willing participants to role play a historical period that has come up in someone's life. You then move to an open discussion on where you could research background information for life stories. You have a Powerpoint presentation to share with the participants or a handout that they can take away with them for future use. Finally, you have a questions and answers session.

This mixture of elements will ensure that there is an activity to suit everyone. You can be creative as you like in delivering a workshop by coming up with new and exciting ways for participants to share in your knowledge and skills whilst gaining some of their own.

Designing a Course

Being a writing tutor is a rewarding and stimulating experience. You are sharing your gift with others who in turn will become writers. You can introduce people to the world of writing whether they want to write for pleasure or for profit.

And the journey through any course you deliver is exciting. You get to meet new people who are willing to give your lessons a go. They put their trust in your hands that the course will be a good one. You have to do your best to find different ways to make writing fun and interesting to learn. This helps you to develop as a tutor and also as a writer.

The key elements of designing a course are time, venue, content and materials. Time management can be an issue for new tutors especially when they have a day job or are writing to a deadline. You can plan ahead for busy times by deciding what time you have to give to tutoring. Tutoring typically runs to school terms. September and January are times when new courses often start. Classes run in the daytime as well as in the evenings. What time suits you best?

The length of a course depends on you and to some extent your students. You may be asked to give a set course that already has a timeframe and course materials but if not, you will need to plan your courses duration. Six weeks is a taster or introductory course, eight weeks gives the subject a little more depth and 16 weeks takes more commitment. Each session is going to be like a workshop and between 2 and 3 hours long. The difference is that each session leads to the next and there is an overall learning experience as well as specific sessions.

Content is key. The course needs a title, an overall aim and a decision on what each session will cover. Each session will need to be timed and thought out like a workshop so that participants are kept interested and involved in the course. Session plans are easy to compile and will give you a schedule to follow. Using a spreadsheet or table, you can map out exactly what you are going to do in each session and how long it will take. You can also note what you will need for each session and anything that you will expect the participants to bring in.

If you are selecting a venue, it needs to be accessible and comfortable. Prospective students can be put off from ever doing a course if these basic elements are not in place. There should be good parking facilities, ramps for wheelchair users and access to toilets and to refreshments. The room used should be comfortably warm with adequate seating and good lighting and ventilation. If you are thinking of delivering a course in a certain venue, check out the different rooms to decide which is the most suitable before you start your course.

Depending on the venue you use and your own preferences will determine what you need. You can get away with as little as yourself and pens and paper for your learners but you can make your course more interesting by using other things. Whiteboards, flipcharts and overhead projectors are regularly used by tutors to give presentations. Dressing-up boxes and props can be used for role-play. Those with access to technology might like to use interactive whiteboards and Powerpoint presentations projected via laptops or use computers as a learning tool during a session. The equipment you use is up to you and you need not complicate it if you'd just prefer to use the basics. Consider what materials are needed at the planning stage and you will have covered any necessities that may come up.

Delivering a Course

No tutor is perfect but you can aim to be! A good tutor

- Listens
- Understands
- Lets their students talk more than they do
- Makes learning fun
- Imparts knowledge in a friendly way
- Is approachable

Gone are the days of ruling a class with an iron fist. To be a tutor today, you have to be a people person. You are going to be working with people who are adults just like you. They don't want to be talked down to or be made to feel they are ignorant. They want to learn something new and have fun doing so.

You have to be able to listen to your students, adapt to their learning styles and respond to their needs. You will have session plans but they should remain flexible. Your group of participants may need more time on one area and less on another and you as their tutor need to go with the group flow. Always have extra resources like handouts or exercises that you can give to fast learners so that they do not get bored waiting for the group to catch up and be ready to support slower learners by giving them an extra 10 mins of your time and extra support after the session.

One thing you will need to impart to students is confidence. Confidence in yourself as a tutor, and confidence in their ability to complete your course. If you've been writing away for years in your lonely turret away from the world, teaching a group of people will hit you with a bang. The thing about confidence is you gain it from doing the very thing you fear. You will be nervous the first time you teach a group but it will pass and you will feel more and more comfortable and at ease and ultimately a better tutor when you gain confidence.

Here's the thing about confidence. You can be it even if you don't feel it! Dress well, not in a suit, but in something smart that makes you feel good. Buy yourself a new bag or folder for materials (retail therapy is a confidence booster!). Be prepared. You will have no need to worry then. Take rescue remedy if you need to calm your nerves. Arrive in plenty of time to feel comfortable in your surroundings. Hold your chin up as it releases mood enhancing endorphins and breathe, long, deep calming breaths. Repeat positive mantras to yourself like 'I can do this' and 'I am a great tutor'.

Positive body language will also give you self-confidence and show your students that you are an open and warm tutor. Students will be as nervous as you starting a new course. There is anticipation of what is to come, whether they will like their tutor and for some, if they have not studied in some time or had a bad learning experience at school, entering your course can be a nerve-wrecking experience. Welcome your students with a smile on your face and open and relaxed body language.

When you are working with the group, be aware of how you use your body and tone of voice. A slumped posture shows apathy, crossed arms show defensiveness. You want to sit alert but relaxed, lean forward when a student is talking to you and nod your head to show agreement and understanding. When you are talking, make good eye-contact. Look at all of your learners and do not focus on anyone in particular. Speak to the group and not the back of the room or out of the window.

Help your participants to feel confident in their own abilities by showing enthusiasm about their work. When your group is working on something, do your rounds. Walk around the group, kneeling down to give words of encouragement and leaving them with a light touch on the back or the arm as a sign of praise and approval. We all look for encouragement and as a tutor it is one of the most important gifts you can give. Making sure you are an approachable and supportive tutor will make your course a success.

Where to Talk and Tutor

So where could you deliver workshops and courses? The most obvious place to start is in your own community. Are there groups that would like to learn new skills and would welcome a tutor? It could be a local women's group or an active retirement group. Is there a community center where people meet up looking for educational opportunities? Or perhaps a local college who are looking for tutors? There are many groups and organizations that could be approached with the idea of a course.

There could be fee paying opportunities where you get paid a tutor's hourly rate or you could hire a room and deliver a course privately, charging participants a set fee for the courses duration. Out of this you will have to pay rental, supply refreshments and materials, but it is possible to also earn an income from delivering your own courses.

Look at where you could rent a room. Hotels can be expensive but will provide all the facilities that you need. Less costly are rooms in community buildings. Church halls or meeting rooms might be available. Find out what is on offer in your area and visit each possibility to check out the rooms, prices and facilities.

Some tutors teach out of their own homes but taking this

route depends on how private you want to keep your home life. If participants know where you live, expect to be contacted at all hours and asked for support when you are not tutoring. You have to be very clear on your boundaries and working hours to manage this effectively.

Wherever you chose to tutor, enjoy the experience. You are a writer with the skills and knowledge to pass onto others. Help other people to tell their tales and bring their stories to life.

Further Reading

Life Writing

The Arvon Book of Life Writing by Carole Angier and Sally Cline

Your Life, Your Story: Writing your Life Story for Family and Friends by Cherry Gilchrist

Bite Size Pieces of My Past: Writing your Life Story in Digestible Chunks by Andrea Bargsley Vincent

Family History

Track down your Ancestors by Estelle Catlett

Ancestral Trails by Mark D Herber

Tracing Your Family History on the Internet by Chris Paton

Family History: Digging Deeper by Simon Fowler

Family History for Beginners by Kirstyanne Ross

Writing Biographies

Writing Biographies: Historians and their Craft by Lloyd E Ambrosius

Complete Guide to Writing Biographies by Ted Schwarz

Writing Biography & Autobiography by Brian D Osborne

Writing For Magazines

Writing for Magazines by Adele Ramet

Writing For Magazines by Jill Dick

Writing For Magazines by Catriona Ross

**COMPASS
BOOKS**

Compass Books focuses on practical and informative 'how-to' books for writers. Written by experienced authors who also have extensive experience of tutoring at the most popular creative writing workshops, the books offer an insight into the more specialised niches of the publishing game.